T0294613

TRANSFORMING INCLUSION IN MUSEUMS

American Alliance of Museums

The American Alliance of Museums has been bringing museums together since 1906, helping to develop standards and best practices, gathering and sharing knowledge, and providing advocacy on issues of concern to the entire museum community. Representing more than thirty-five thousand individual museum professionals and volunteers, institutions, and corporate partners serving the museum field, the Alliance stands for the broad scope of the museum community.

The American Alliance of Museums' mission is to champion museums and nurture excellence in partnership with its members and allies.

Books published by AAM further the Alliance's mission to make standards and best practices for the broad museum community widely available.

TRANSFORMING INCLUSION IN MUSEUMS

The Power of Collaborative Inquiry

Porchia Moore, Rose Paquet, and Aletheia Wittman

ROWMAN & LITTLEFIELD
Lanham • Boulder • New York • London

Published by Rowman & Littlefield
An imprint of The Rowman & Littlefield Publishing Group, Inc.
4501 Forbes Boulevard, Suite 200, Lanham, Maryland 20706
www.rowman.com

86-90 Paul Street, London EC2A 4NE

British Library Cataloguing in Publication Information Available

Library of Congress Cataloging-in-Publication Data

Names: Moore, Porchia, 1978- author. | Paquet, Rose, 1984- author. |
    Wittman, Aletheia, 1987- author. | American Alliance of Museums.
Title: Transforming inclusion in museums : the power of collaborative inquiry / Porchia
    Moore, Rose Paquet, and Aletheia Wittman.
Description: Lanham : Rowman & Littlefield, [2022] | Publication supported by the
    American Alliance of Museums. | Includes bibliographical references and index. |
    Summary: "This book proposes that the Incluseum's paradigm can help the field meet
    the challenges of this current landscape and offer practical guidance for museum
    workers, leaders and emerging professionals doing the daily work to transform the
    future of museums"— Provided by publisher.
Identifiers: LCCN 2022003713 (print) | LCCN 2022003714 (ebook) | ISBN
    9781538161890 (cloth ; alk. paper) | ISBN 9781538161906 (pbk ; alk. paper) | ISBN
    9781538161913 (electronic)
Subjects: LCSH: Museums and minorities—United States. | Incluseum (Project) |
    Museums—Social aspects—United States. | Museums and community—United States.
    | Organizational change—United States.
Classification: LCC AM11 .M66 2022 (print) | LCC AM11 (ebook) | DDC 069—dc23/
    eng/20220215
LC record available at https://lccn.loc.gov/2022003713
LC ebook record available at https://lccn.loc.gov/2022003714

Contents

Acknowledgments

WITHIN ALL OUR RESPECTIVE WORK, and as individuals, we strive to build a ritual and practice of thanks and acknowledgment for those who came before us and work beside us. In honesty, we feel overwhelmed by the support we have received over the years. We thank our families, our friends, and our communities, who believed in us and in our work with *The Incluseum* project over the past ten years. Your support is what made this project and book possible.

It has been our goal, not just here but throughout the writing of this book, to recognize the many who have influenced our work and thinking and who we have worked with directly. Many of these individuals will be acknowledged in depth in chapter 1. The work of many more will be referenced and cited as sources. We hope you read the full acknowledgment of *Incluseum* blog authors that can be found at the end of this book in the appendix. To each of these contributors, we thank you.

We would like to extend special gratitude to Margaret Middleton and nikhil trivedi. As regular contributors, collaborators, and trusted advisors, we have relied on them at many points over the past decade to assess whether we are going in the right direction. They have been models for us. We have learned how to expand our individual and collective thinking about inclusion because of their labor and time and by virtue of being in community with them. Thank you.

Preface

A S WE HAVE COMPLETED THIS BOOK, our collective realities as authors, and *The Incluseum*'s codirectors, have no doubt mirrored many of your realities these past two years (2020–2022):

- supporting friends facing health challenges,
- grieving deaths of community members due to the COVID-19 pandemic,
- research plans scrapped—reformulated to respond to a shifting landscape,
- layoffs,
- new jobs,
- economic instability,
- political instability,
- caring for children,
- heartbreaks,
- the collective grieving of continued police brutality and social injustices,
- the continued global impacts of extreme weather/climate events,
- moving cross-country,
- the transformation of work as we knew it, and
- the transformation of our outlook onto what museums are and ought to be in this new emerging reality.

The question, as we see it, is *how* will we respond to the transformation we are going through. Are we ready to open ourselves up to this transformation? How should we approach this process? This book offers insights in response to these questions rooted in what we have learned from *The Incluseum* project over the past decade.

The Incluseum project was an idea Rose and Aletheia had in 2012 that provided a solution to what we perceived to be a gap or a problem. The problem was that there was no central resource to chronicle and build community around new approaches to understanding inclusion in museums, a gap Rose and Aletheia were experiencing firsthand as they did graduate work at the University of Washington Museology Program (2010–2012). Scholarship and practice addressing inclusion felt scattered, siloed, inaccessible, and underprioritized in museum discourse. We started a blog as a way to invite museum practitioners and museum-adjacent partners to help us build a conversation and *a space to center* collaborative inquiry about inclusion. We used social media platforms to share what we wrote and to connect with people we could invite to write for the blog. The timing was right. Many museum practitioners and scholars who had been developing their own ideas and practices for years wanted a community to talk about inclusion in museums. One of these amazing practitioners who connected with *The Incluseum* in its earliest years, Dr. Porchia Moore, now completes our team of *Incluseum* codirectors. When Porchia first connected with *The Incluseum* (2013) she was pursuing her doctoral work at the University of South Carolina.

As *The Incluseum* project continued to evolve, Rose and Aletheia worked on projects based in Seattle (where we lived) that could serve as opportunities to put evolving ideas about inclusion into practice. First, *The Incluseum* launched a digital exhibit titled *The Power of Labeling* (2014) with the help of exhibit advisors and University of Washington Museology students.[1] *The Incluseum* also launched a community-specific art installation titled *The Power of Place* (2015).[2] Rose went on to do doctoral work at the University of Washington's Information School, developing an Incluseum Design Workshop in 2014. Since then, Rose, Porchia, and Aletheia have run the workshop with different student groups, at museum conferences, and as a facilitation tool at various museums over the years. And, in 2015, Rose, Porchia, and Aletheia started supporting and advising the MASS Action project launched by Elisabeth Callihan at the Minneapolis Institute of Art (MASS Action will be discussed in greater depth in chapter 1). These *Incluseum* collaborations have been ways to learn through doing as much as thinking, writing, and organizing. We feel proud of our work on each of these projects, but the process of learning through these projects is what we value most. Each collaboration has been a means to grapple with praxis (where our ideas meet practice) and to seek new understanding through contextual and relational accountability.

This book sets out to differ from *and* expand on our work to date with *The Incluseum*. It also strives for a degree of continuity, to uphold the values and character for which *The Incluseum* has come to be known. *The Incluseum* blog has built a reputation over the years as a platform to find inquisitive, trustworthy, analytical, and nuanced perspectives on inclusion as a concept and a set of practices enacted within museums. We take the responsibility of this reputation seriously. We are in a relationship of accountability to you, the reader, and by extension all who trust our platform and believe in what it has come to stand for. In this spirit, we want to take this opportunity to clearly situate ourselves as authors and name our decisions about language and the writing process, aspects of this book that might not be immediately, or ever, apparent for you, the reader, otherwise.

First, we have made some intentional language choices to refer to groups excluded from museums. These are:

- **Historically Marginalized:** No matter how you slice it, the structure of museums, and those who lead them, operates from a place of marginalizing and codifying the marginalized as well as using power to marginalize.
- **Historically Underrepresented:** Indicative of a *pattern* of underrepresentation, not just current underrepresentation. It suggests the exclusions and discrimination precipitating being underrepresented as well as an evaluation of the representation a group experiences (that it is under the amount it should be).
- **Historically Disengaged:** Indicative of a past in which no relationship has been established with a group. It suggests disinterest of a group due to the irrelevance of a museum.
- **People of the Global Majority:** A critical term first introduced to us by PGM One, a BIPOC-centered project that is part of the Earth Institute, that pronounces the reality that people of color represent the numerical majority in the world's population. In addition, this term alludes to the relationship between power and perceptions of power between melanated and less melanated peoples.

We especially think that it becomes increasingly important to recognize this final term and the impending historical, political, and socioeconomic repercussions as the US Census Bureau recently reported that for the first time ever there is a shrinkage in the "White-only" population. This report is actually much more complicated than issues of race and is more about shifting notions of identity. In our field, as in society at large, we have long patterned our thinking in terms of dichotomies. We tend to think in terms of racialized groups: Black, White, Latinx, etc. Yet the steady increase in bi- or multiracial identities means that as our world continues to expand so must our thinking about racial identities and inclusion. We lean on this term, People of the Global Majority, as a way to expand our understanding of power and to hold ourselves accountable for unlearning the ways in which this nation's complicated language regarding race requires continual explication and interrogation (US Census, 2021).

Likewise, it occurs to us that—at the same time as an individual might identify with a historically marginalized, underrepresented, or disengaged group—an individual might also identify with groups who form another global majority, or an otherwise well-represented population in society, such as people who live with a disability or people experiencing poverty. So we acknowledge that within these excluded groups are broader, deeper, and specific histories and relationships that themselves require our attention beyond a framework that uses the museum as the sole reference point for understanding group exclusion.

Second, we often have cause within this book to refer to clusters, or acronyms, of key concepts because they are often understood and discussed in relation to each other. For example, we use the acronym DEAI (diversity, equity, accessibility, and inclusion) in our discussion of the genealogy of inclusion in US museums. And we will use another acronym, IEAJ (inclusion, equity, accessibility, and justice), to refer to a collection of concepts that we feel have particular significance within our own approach to inclusion and the one we understand to be most critical for the museum field's attention today. There might not be a "right" acronym; these inevitably reflect and communicate evolving understanding of the shifting and growing process of finding the language to suit our times.

Another similarity that carries over to this book from our work with *The Incluseum* online is its coauthorship format. We (Rose, Porchia, and Aletheia) took alternating leads on developing each respective chapter; this included drafting chapters and outlines, sharing them, and coediting each other's work. We worked when we could, met whenever we could, but kept flexible to honor each other's schedule and capacity. Editing happened iteratively, through in-person discussion and inquiry about each other's ideas. For the reader, we imagine that this means there might be moments where our distinct voices shine through within what might be read as our collective ("we") voice. Deciding to write in this fashion felt natural because of our years working on *The Incluseum* together. It is familiar to us, and yet we acknowledge that it is a fairly unusual or uncommon voice to establish in a work of creative nonfiction. We want to acknowledge that, despite the familiarity we have with this mode of working, a book written this way is practically impossible without deep care and trust of each other.

As facilitators of *The Incluseum*, we have sometimes been content authors, often been editors and collaborators, and frequently been amplifiers. In addition to these roles, although not always consciously or explicitly stated, we have been space makers. We created the platform in 2012. We cultivated a sense of place around it; our agency as individuals has been expressed (maybe even felt?) through our early claiming of a mission statement and a vision for the project and through our intentional and invitational engagement with contributors. In the introduction, we will delve deeper into the beliefs that developed over time and have guided our work with *The Incluseum* project and shaped the identity of the platform.

At the same time, we have also sought to decentralize and redistribute how knowledge about inclusion is produced and represented through *The Incluseum*. We, as facilitators, have been but one partner in the relationship by which we endeavored to build collective understanding of inclusion in museums; the other partner in this project is *you*. So we have felt responsible to you to share what we have learned from this project over time. Likewise, we want to know:

- How do our learnings overlap with your own or put words to experiences you too have lived?
- How does your realm of museum practice bring the insights we offer into focus?
- How do our attempts to convey our learnings fall short of the fullness of your own experiences?

While a book is less suited than a blog for a two-way dynamic, this book is necessarily a continuation in an ongoing dialogue *and* an opportunity for this dialogue to reach new audiences. The platform we have tried to cultivate through our facilitation, coordination, and imagining with *The Incluseum* over the years is the "hometown" where this book project grew up. Whether we met you through the blog, in person, or are meeting you through this coauthored book, we hope *The Incluseum* offers you a place to feel connected with others in our shared work of inquiry and imagining.

Notes

1. With gratitude to our exhibition advisors Erin Bailey-Sun, Davida Ingram, Dave Kennedy, and Zachary Stocks, as well as our interns Jana Greenslit and Sarah Taggart. See incluseum.com/exhibits/.

2. See incluseum.com/exhibits/.

Bibliography

US Census Bureau. "2020 Census Statistics Highlight Local Population Changes and Nation's Racial and Ethnic Diversity." https://www.census.gov/newsroom/press -releases/2021/population-changes-nations-diversity.html.

Introduction

Our Original Musing

*W*HAT IS INCLUSION IN MUSEUMS? This is the question we started asking separately, and then collectively. This question had an urgency. Rose arrived at this question after working in community-based museums, then discovering more exclusionary realities outside of these spaces. Aletheia was encountering the many ways emerging curatorial practices engage with social justice as a pathway to address legacies of museum exclusion. Porchia arrived at this work deeply frustrated by the lack of scholarship and critical analysis of institutional racism in museums. We knew museums to be exclusive in many ways, shapes, and forms. This, it seemed, was the starting place. So what was the antidote to these storied and lasting patterns of exclusion? Where were the museum practitioners who were asking similar critical questions of the field and intervening through their practice? Did others in the field see and feel the gaps in access to resources and examples regarding inclusion?

As cultural scholars and workers ourselves, the stakes of answering these questions felt high. We wanted to resist replicating the practices that continued to consolidate power in existing, exclusive museum practices and structures. We needed to stretch our imagination. We wanted to put aside any presupposed limitations to museum practice and fix our attention on something new, an *Incluseum*.

This idea of an *Incluseum* proposed a future reality. *The Incluseum* project was our intervention, to claim a site for world building—a literal website—where we and other cultural workers could inquire about inclusion collectively.

The project has functioned like a web, cross-connecting a growing number of cultural workers interrogating existing practices and paradigms, language and frameworks—an Inclusive Museum Movement (Moore, 2016). *The Incluseum* became a springboard for grassroots understandings of inclusion but also for new notions of what it means to be a museum altogether.

Due to the sheer scale of published content and the temporal distance between entries, it is not immediately apparent to a casual reader or contributor what we have learned from *The Incluseum* project—until now. And so, a decade later, we look backward, forward, and side to side at what an "insurgent museum project" (Quinn, 2016, p. 11) can tell us about inclusion and the future of museums.

Museum Love Stories

Every museum professional can usually tell you three things: (1) what their favorite museums are, (2) why they entered the field, and (3) a list of things they wish they could change about either their museum, the field, or both. Perhaps after a packed day of inspiring conference panels and keynotes at an annual museum conference or sitting around a table or a bar while at a Drinking About Museums event someone will ask the question, "What is your first museum experience?" You might witness two dozen museum professionals close their eyes and think hard, seeing flashes of memory as they recall the first time they entered a museum and with whom. They will recall how that visit made them feel, what they could touch, or what was behind a glass case or rope that made them stop and stare for some unspecified amount of time. They will speak in great detail about the joys, the questions, the excitement of falling in love with museums. They will share about an unspeakable desire to connect to a particular institution or a revelation that a desire to work in a museum someday likely began at that very moment. Inevitably, the question can be viewed as one of significant importance because, in reality, what is being asked is a question about love. A museum love story, if you will. What is it about museums that so many of us dedicate our lives to? In fact, for some museum professionals, the love story has a different origin. There is first a love for community and a desire to change the ways in which museums function because that first museum encounter felt more like rage or disappointment. That feeling that their community or their people deserved more lit a fire in their hearts for change. What is the source of the passion that we hold for museums in a profession that is in need of major change, that has undergone significant transformation and turmoil, and that often offers huge rewards and often far less pay than we deserve?

One day we asked the question of one another: "When did you first fall in love with museums?" It sent us on a journey that helped us locate memories deep within ourselves and connect us to the work that we have dedicated the past couple decades of our lives to. We found it important to go back to our origin stories, if you will, to our beginnings to examine the roots of our work as a means of expanding the frame for our ongoing scholarship, examination, interrogation, and critique of museums. When you love something, you want the best for it and you want it to grow, prosper, and flourish, or else die and be reincarnated as a better version of itself. This is our desire for museums.

Our critical questions are propositions for reshaping and reimagining—for breathing new life into an institution and a profession rooted in harmful colonialist ideologies. We collectively found that our origin, or love stories were really about belonging. A deep sense of belonging and identity. A whimsy. A gnawing. A live-wired current running along our spines where we saw the importance of education, inquiry, fun and play, and connecting with our loved ones—the ongoing gift of a museum visit. With that, over the past decade, *The Incluseum* as a project has been a labor of love, a platform created to share stories and experiences, ask critical questions, and push our collective thinking and practice. In the process, it has also become a dreamspace and a brain trust of ideas and resources reaching thousands of readers across the globe.

As *The Incluseum* project developed over time, it became clear that the project was not just about an exploration of a single word—inclusion—it was about creating a place, an *Incluseum*, that could evoke a powerful sense of belonging. Inclusion and belonging are both tied to the notion of "being held" and being held gently and with compassion. What is love, if not that? In our respective journeys in the field as professionals and in our lives as visitors we wanted to unpack and clarify if and how enacting inclusion could eradicate exclusion. We view exclusion as the umbrella for all of the -isms and barriers to the field for professionals and to participation for visitors. Our love story, then, is focused on understanding inclusion and how it can expand all of our collective belonging.

Letting a Word Lead Us

If a picture is worth a thousand words, then is a single word worth a thousand blogposts? Tweets? "Inclusion." A decade ago that word was barely used in the US museum field. Diversity was the word of the day, just barely eclipsed by other coded terms such as multiculturalism or accessibility (Moore, 2014). Take, for example, Emily Kotecki, who has created a brilliant podcast called

Museum Buzz (see @museumbuzz1). Each episode, Kotecki asks insightful thought leaders and creatives in our field to explore a single word. The podcast is a meditative, fun exploration of the language and rhetoric museum professionals use on a daily basis. What do we mean when we use terms such as "community," "diversity," "social justice," "virtual learning," and more? Outside of the field, any of these buzzwords potentially take on a new meaning. Yet within the context of museums each of these words or any word deemed "buzzy" has the ability to refocus and/or problematize our best practices. They challenge our understanding of how and why we do things in the field. And so it is with *The Incluseum* and our eagle-eyed focus on inclusion. The project is titled *The Incluseum* because we felt strongly that inclusion was an umbrella term that, rather than having a short-term impact within the field, had far-reaching if not permanent implications of critical importance for where we believed the field needed to expand and aspire. More than the opposite of exclusion, we understood inclusion to be a concept full of potential for addressing a multitude of concerns plaguing the field, including and not limited to

- lack of BIPOC leadership in museums,
- issues with BIPOC retention in the field,
- lack of participation from BIPOC visitors,
- inequity caused by unpaid internships,
- a failure to adequately expand and apply disability and accessibility frameworks,
- lack of promoting and centralizing LGBQTI2+ leadership and histories,
- gross disparities in salaries between museum leadership and other professionals,
- inaccurate or poor interpretation of material culture,
- the fallacies of professionalism that failed to address legacies of White supremacist work cultures, and
- institutional and systemic racism and more.

The concept of buzzwords is that they endure repeated use over a short period of time to the point that some or most of the original intent behind the word is lost, muted, or changed in some manner. There is a time stamp on buzzwords as the problem or situation associated with the word is either resolved, glossed over, or no longer holds our attention. We felt strongly that there was something significant about inclusion, that it held an endurance over time and operated as a functional way to problem solve. In addition, we believed that there were opportunities to nuance and expand on inclusion to unlock its deeply imaginative potential. We see our work as imaginative, expansive, and participatory. Therefore, as a collaborative project, the platform is designed to allow museum workers to explore the dimensions of inclusion beyond mere rhetoric and to solidify the term as a valuable framework for our field. While buzzwords are often associated with showcasing a familiarity with language used in a profession, they are not often fully defined and critical principles are not usually applied. In the ten years that we have interrogated inclusion, contributors to the project have taken a single word and fleshed it out to give meaning, nuance, and applicable insights to the entire field, that is, museum studies and the professional sector of museums and cultural heritage. And so we let a single word lead us into a global dialogue on space making, leadership, activism, racial equity, and change. We practiced deep listening and centered collaborative inquiry and community building as principles in motion for the platform to flourish. We see and continue to view vast promise in what was once considered "buzzy."

From Digital to Print

It is not lost on us that *The Incluseum* is a born-digital project, residing on the internet—a project that spans global time zones and connects thousands of readers. In the first several years of the project, social media platforms such as Facebook and Twitter were powerful tools to connect to new contributors, build a network of readers, and expand the platform's reach. When the project started in 2012 as a blog and website it was a base for intentionally and consistently weaving together a web of voices and ideas pertaining to inclusion in museums in the public realm—free for all to access and inviting to all who might imagine themselves a partner in weaving this web with us. This web of voices and ideas began to take on its own form, significance, and meaning beyond us and our seed of an idea. That *The Incluseum*, a born-digital space, could develop attributes through collective visioning and collaborative inquiry—becoming a world of its own—was unimaginable then. Ten years later, we find that this digital platform served as an excellent incubator for community building, bringing together both digital and offline engagements (*The Incluseum*, 2012). The strength of the web that we wove in the digital sphere translated fairly naturally to offline community connections. That community spurred new and side collaborations.

Coming to understand the power of a digital project offering free content—including printable, shareable resources and tools—has been one of the most satisfying parts of *The Incluseum* project. In 2020, we saw the museum world "pivot" to digital content in an unprecedented way and rapidly develop "hybrid" (in-person and online) models for engagement. With attention, time, experimentation, and energy, the digital life of museums large and small grew. Most of this new digital museum content has been free, taking the place of the physical museum "experience" as the main museum offering. While backgrounded by the grief of a pandemic that isolated us in different ways, museums made strides in accessibility and virtual event production and reached a remote audience ready to engage. *The Incluseum*'s decade-long experience facilitating a digital platform, inextricably linked to offline community and in-person engagements, seems particularly pertinent to reflect on as we witness museums on a field-wide scale navigating a hybrid mode for the foreseeable future, considering the lasting impacts of the COVID-19 pandemic, and embracing the power of digital place making in building communities and relationships that bridge the in-person and the digital realms.

So why move to print now? Print allows us the space to chronicle the collective wisdom accrued on *The Incluseum* digital platform over the past ten years and to engage new audiences. The tactility of the printed page, we hope, evokes a new kind of creative energy—the potential for blank pages to become filled with new notes, new questions, and new musings. In addition, we hope to disrupt our own patterns of learning and knowing by making a new offering. Change is vital for growth. And while we do not subscribe to the notion that the written word, or the academy only, legitimizes knowledge and represents the full spectrum of necessary and valid knowledge, translating our born-digital project to print has been a means to stretch our thinking and share the fruits of our collective web weaving.

What This Book Is and Is Not

This book is a celebration of *The Incluseum* project and the fruits of the collaborative inquiry that it has catalyzed to date. It is designed to present a powerful look at what we have learned and what you have taught us through your sharing, reading, writing, and digital participation over the past ten years about the value and practice of inclusion. It is a celebration of our contributors and readers and how this brain trust of museum professionals across the world has activated vital shifts in our field.

It is a book that summarizes, synthesizes, and archives a genealogy of inclusion in US museums including a burgeoning movement, The Inclusive Museum Movement (chapter 1), and delves into the limits of the concept as it is used today (chapter 2). This book shares a thematic analysis of *The Incluseum* content archive and synthesizes findings into a new paradigm for understanding inclusion that can open us up to necessary and timely transformation (chapter 3) and introduces the implications and uses of such a paradigm for the museum field in an era of uprising and upheaval (chapter 4). In our final chapter (chapter 5), we call for a complete reorientation of the field's understanding of inclusion moving forward.

The book arrives at a crucial junction. It comes at a time when a global pandemic has threatened the cultural heritage sector and terms such as "diversity," "equity," "access," "social justice," and "inclusion" went from ubiquitous buzzwords and purported necessary values to being included in policies, statements, and trainings to being challenged and even outlawed.

This book is not a magic wand. It is not a step-by-step guide to ending institutional racism or even a workbook for solving every problem in the field or your institution. This book is not a means of saying we have all of the answers (we don't). This book is a purposeful analysis and accountability for the collective work that we have done as a project toward understanding, expanding, working toward, and achieving inclusion. Most critically, it is an attempt to ask the hard questions on the progress that we have made in our field regarding diversity, equity, access, and social justice as an output of inclusive praxis. Doing the work means that each individual museum commits to the transformation required for each unique, locally situated community. There are no blanket strategies or techniques. For every museum exists a unique plan for inclusion. What inclusion looks like for one community will look vastly different for another.

This book does not reinforce current and previous standards of "best practices" for museum work. This book is a call to action. We deserve a new paradigm for inclusion in service of antiracist institutions dedicated to new ways of being and leaning heavily on new ways of knowing—trusting in the knowledge and wisdom we have created in these past ten years. We want Incluseums!

How to Read This Book

Take notes. Take photos. Write in the margins. Color code. Screenshot. Share. Post on social media. We want this book to be well worn and have the feel of a workbook, the tone of a passionate accomplice, and the historical archival memory and analysis of memory workers, activist-scholars, and practitioners. The main way to read this book is in communication with the following:

a. *The Incluseum* blog (past, present, and future posts)
b. Current media and content regarding race, inclusion, and museums
c. The Museum Twitterverse (join in any number of conversations and threads regarding museums)
d. In community

Read this book with an open mind. We hope that even if you have been a contributor, have followed *The Incluseum*'s journey these past ten years, feel well read about the work of IEAJ in museums, or are actively leading inclusion work in your own museums that you will still learn something new. We intend for this book to read as a primer and a reference tool. We envision it as a kind of historiography and a map for the journey ahead.

What We Believe In

We believe that museums have the ability to sustain and educate our communities in new ways. We believe that the museum field is full of brilliant, capable people who deserve excellence in leadership, who can be excellent leaders, and who benefit from new ideas and creative solution-driven strategies for transformative praxis. Therefore we do not view ourselves as content creators but facilitators, activist-scholars, and practitioners. We believe in collaboration. Creating and sharing ideas. We believe in the wisdom of the collective. Always.

We work in a particular way that has continued to develop over time and we feel that it is necessary to outline our values:

Incluseum Values and Guiding Principles

Critical Dialogue
- We believe that disruption is a powerful tool for learning and growth.
- We are nourished by the intuitive power of curiosity.
- We are not tied to best practices, outmoded notions of professionalism, and common ways of doing things just because.
- We aspire to the courage and freedom to learn new things.
- We believe that action should be responsive, not reactive.
- We learn through engaging with one another.

Community Building
- We grow through the wisdom of the collective.
- We understand there is no one-size-fits-all approach to inclusion, and intensive labor is required to manifest a path toward inclusive practice.
- We uplift and acknowledge ways of knowing and working outside of current museum standards.
- We approach partnership with sincerity, authenticity, and truth.
- We create and share tools because they facilitate the exchange of ideas and are necessary for the expansion of community.

Collaborative Practice
- We work together.
- We invest our time, labor, and attention in innovation and ideas.
- We move freely between honoring urgency and respecting the need for slow learning and active listening as a model for cultural responsiveness.
- We trust in the potential of shared knowledges to correct/restore.

We believe we can all benefit from a community in which innovative and experimental approaches to museum practice, curiosity, questions, successes, and failures are amplified to help us collectively approximate the solutions most suitable in our own contexts and the future we want for the field and our workplaces.

Inclusion is a collaborative, multimodal, expansive, and inquisitive process.

This shared visioning work is indebted to, and an outgrowth of, its deep roots in conversations, collaboration, movements, and individual activism begun many decades earlier. In the following chapter, we turn to these precursors to situate *The Incluseum* within the broader, ongoing story of influential moments that have shaped and continue to shape how we understand inclusion in the US museum field.

Key Questions

1. What is your museum love story?
2. What do you know for sure needs to change about museums for both museum professionals and their visitors?
3. What is your vision for museums and what tools, conditions, information, or leadership styles do you need to realize this vision?
4. What are your personal values and how or where are these values supported in your institution?
5. In what ways have you contributed to the global digital community of museum professionals and what was its impact?

Bibliography

Moore, Porchia. "The Danger of the 'D' Word: Museums and Diversity." *The Incluseum*. January 20, 2014. https://incluseum.com/2014/01/20/the-danger-of-the-d-word-museums-and-diversity/.

Moore, Porchia. "The Inclusive Museum Movement." *Museum*, November/December 2016.

The Incluseum. "Vision Statement." 2012. https://incluseum.com/about/.

Quinn, Therese. "Welcome." Issue #1 Inaugurations. *FWD: Museums*, 2016.

1

What Is Inclusion?

A Genealogy of Inclusion in US Museums

I N THIS CHAPTER, WE DEVELOP a genealogy of inclusion in US museums.
This genealogical work helps us trace back—and forward—different influential moments that have shaped contemporary understandings of inclusion in the field. This account emerges from the authors' collective memory, research, and dialogue, but, as all accounts go, is partial. We encourage you, the reader, to consider other aspects and forces that we might have unintentionally omitted.

Tracing the roots of inclusion in US museums takes us several decades back to the 1960s and the emergence of community- and culturally specific museums in the civil rights, or the "second reconstruction," era. This is followed by the theoretical contributions of the New Museology in the late 1980s and the development of social inclusion theory in the late 1990s in the United Kingdom. This genealogical work then brings us back to the United States when in the 2010s the US museum field saw a flurry of activities pertaining to inclusion. We will first discuss AAM's uptake of corporate diversity and inclusion language to formulate its first definition of inclusion in 2014. Next, we will look at how practitioner pushback and activism contributed to AAM reconsidering inclusion within a more comprehensive framework called Diversity, Equity, Access, and Inclusion (DEIA) in 2018. Finally, we will highlight the significant role of grassroots activist projects and initiatives in shaping the US museum field's contemporary understanding of inclusion from a justice-centered perspective. Overall, these projects and initiatives provide ongoing pushback, depth, substance, and accountability to discourses of inclusion and DEIA in the field.

A Community Museum Movement

Community museums (also referred to as culturally specific or neighborhood museums) have long been an embodiment of ground-up inclusion efforts—amplifying counter-narratives, heritage, culture, and local knowledge. In the midst of the civil rights movement of the 1960s, museums too were a mode of making and claiming space as well as representation—necessitated by long-standing erasure of community-based knowledges within the dominant, primarily White, US museum system. Within this broader movement, sub-movements mobilized, like the Black Museum Movement (Burns, 2013). Notable museums founded in this era and in following decades include Anacostia Community Museum, The Studio Museum, and the Wing Luke Museum. These museums laid the groundwork for the continuing emergence of community museums in the coming decades, like the Chinatown History Museum in New York City. Even before the boom in community museum projects, there were community museum precursors such as the Museum at Hampton University (an HBCU) in 1868 and the Osage Tribal Museum in 1938.[1]

These varied and unique community museum projects serve as radical models for remaking museums by and for communities. However, because of the ways the dominant museum system has received and engaged with the Community Museum Movement, the potential of the movement to shape museum practice broadly has been marginalized and resisted. Rather than recognized as paradigm-shifting projects, instructive to the direction of change in the US museum system, community museums are often "othered" and relegated to their own "type" of museum. The signs of broader institutional shifts in the dominant US museum system have taken decades longer and continued collective efforts since.

New Museology Arrives

Since museums' early days between the birth of the Enlightenment and the end of the colonial period, a time span of roughly 150 years (from approximately 1650 to 1800), museums have engaged in collection, preservation, curation, and exhibition. The collections at the center of these institutions often reflected, and still do, the whims of individual collectors and efforts to amass material wealth during the colonial period. Given this historical legacy, most museums are rooted in the notion that the world can be known and categorized to tell a definitive narrative (Patterson, Wittman, Phillips, Guillotte, Quinn, and Russell, 2017). Academics, curators in particular, have supported this epistemology. As curators sought to best transmit the rational and definitive narrative, they applied themselves to developing "proper" methods for organizing and displaying collections.

The emergence of the New Museology as a theoretical and practice-oriented lens for museums came about as a response to this dominant museo-logical paradigm.[2] It is often ascribed to the 1989 publication of Peter Vergo's germinal work, an edited collection titled *The New Museology*. Vergo aimed to break with what he called the "old museology," a field of theory and prac-tice focused too heavily, in his opinion, on "museum *methods*, and too little about the purposes of museums" (Vergo, 1989, p. 3). According to Vergo, this disproportionate focus on "how to" matters and best practices (that is, museum methods) had, over time, left the assumptions and motivations underlying these methods unexamined and thus undertheorized.

This collection, which was the first of its kind in the field, built on and ampli-fied ideas and debates regarding the political nature of representation that were circulating across various academic disciplines at the time. For museums, this meant that their main activities of collecting and displaying artifacts to represent and speak on behalf of others came under scrutiny and were prob-lematized; these knowledge-producing activities could no longer be carried out under the guise of neutrality (Mason, 2006).[3] In his introduction to the collec-tion, Vergo reminded the readers that, "whether we like it or not, every acquisi-tion (and indeed disposal), every juxtaposition or arrangement of an object or work of art, together with other objects or works of art, within the context of a temporary exhibition or museum display means placing a certain construction upon history" (Vergo, 1989, pp. 2–3). This construction, he clarifies, is shaped by subjective cultural values as to aesthetic, intellectual, and other preferences (p. 2). In other words, the knowledge-producing activities of collecting and displaying artifacts have political, ideological, and aesthetic dimensions, ema-nating from the institution and its legacies, as well as the individuals that make up a particular institution (see also Hooper-Greenhill, 1992; Bennet, 1995; Clifford, 1997). The nonneutral nature of these knowledge-producing activities thus demands that museum professionals do more critical reflection on these activities' contexts and processes (Macdonald, 2006).

Vergo's edited collection also extended one of the motivations that had led to the opening of ecomuseums[4] and other forms of community-based or culturally specific museums discussed earlier. This motivation was that muse-ums should go "from being about something to being for somebody" (Weil, 1999). It's not that museums were for nobody prior to this but that museums were seen to cater to a small, privileged group that did not reflect "the public" museums purported to serve. In other words, museums were called on to become more *visitor centered*, places of enjoyment, leisure, and participation in addition to being places of study and knowledge.

In sum, the New Museology sought to address the role of museums in society, calling on them to become more reflexive, that is, more critical of the assumptions and motivations that underlie their practices and to focus more on people rather than on "how tos" and best practices lest they become "living fossils" (Vergo, 1989, p. 4). This critical turn in museums led to a number of publications that have become key in the field of museology and to the proliferation of educational and community-oriented programming. Since the early work described here, the New Museology has seen a return to "old" museological concerns for methods. This return to how-tos is enriched by the conceptual work developed through the "first wave" of New Museological work (Macdonald, 2006). This focus on practice is crucial if those invested in the New Museology wish to see the changes they have advocated for take place.

The Influence of Social Inclusion

Following the development of the New Museology, the field saw the profusion of initiatives centered on values such as community, democracy, and participation. These initiatives extended and amplified themes brought about by the New Museology, exploring their implication for theory and practice. Within this emergent landscape of public-oriented efforts, the value of inclusion explicitly surfaced in the United Kingdom museum field as social inclusion theory.

In the 1990s, a series of policy moves linked museums to the United Kingdom's greater *social inclusion* policy agenda (Department of Culture, Media, and Sports [DCMS], 1999; 2000a; 2000b; 2005). Through these policy efforts, museums were mandated to address the various barriers that had been identified to prevent people from historically underrepresented groups from accessing museum resources. Moreover, museums were called on to tackle social exclusion occurring on a broader, societal level by linking their services to the four main social exclusion indicators the UK government identified as critical, namely, poor health, high crime, low educational attainment, and unemployment (Sandell, 2003; Tlili, 2012). In the words of Chris Smith, the UK secretary of state in 2000:

> Combating social exclusion is one of the Government's highest priorities, and I believe that museums, galleries and archives have a significant role to play in helping us to do this. They are often the focal point for cultural activity in the community, interpreting its history and heritage. This gives people a sense of their own identity, and that of their community. But the evidence is that museums, galleries and archives can do more than this, and act as agents of social change in the community, improving the quality of people's lives through their outreach activities. (DCMS, 2000a, p. 3)

From this perspective, museums were expected to align themselves with the state's policy agenda and transcend their traditional roles of collecting, preserving, and educating to take on a more *socially purposeful role*, that of acting as *agents of social inclusion* (Sandell, 1998; Tlili, Gewirtz, and Cribb, 2007). In other words, museums were expected to harness their resources and services to help alleviate factors that contribute to social exclusion in their communities, thus delivering positive social outcomes that extend beyond the confines of their four walls.

During the late 1990s and early 2000s, the Museum Studies Department at the University of Leicester undertook notable research projects to help provide insight into museums' links with social exclusion. Sandell (1998; 2002), for example, cited the ways in which museums often promote and affirm dominant values and beliefs as factors contributing to an institutionalized form of social exclusion, a theme that will be echoed in the US museum field's inclusion discourses. He articulated this form of exclusion as particularly problematic as it not only reflects an individual or group's preexisting exclusion from the political, economic, and social realms of society but also perpetuates it (see also Bourdieu, 1993). As a result, Sandell described museums as exacerbating an individual or group's "position of exclusion by broadcasting an exclusive image reinforcing the prejudices and discriminatory practices of museum users and the wider society" (Sandell, 1998, p. 408). Subsequent research projects explored what constitutes barriers to access across UK-based museums, and what approaches address and remedy these barriers (Dodd and Sandell, 2001; Group for Large Local Authority Museums, 2000; Sandell, 2003).

While these insights were primarily UK-based, a number of key publications followed that helped contribute an international perspective to museums' role in society. For example, the edited volume *Museums, Society, Inequality* (Sandell, 2002) brought together international case studies and theoretical insights into social inclusion in museums. This early work was influential to many museum studies students and scholars in the United States, as it presented different approaches to thinking about and working on inclusion in museums.

It is to the US museum field that we turn next. The adoption of inclusion in the United States presents several discontinuities and new directions from the UK context. Aspects that remain the same across contexts, however, are the importance of museums making their resources available to wider segments of the population and having a positive impact on society. The discussion here will clarify this and bring to the fore the context of inclusion in the US museum field.

Inclusion in the US Museum Field

The US museum field's focus on inclusion has intensified over the past decade. It is marked by a diversity of actors and initiatives that have aimed to "inform, educate, and actively pursue the best practices in inclusion" (Shellman, 2019, p. 126). In this section, we highlight some of these initiatives and actors.

a) AAM's 2014 Diversity and Inclusion Policy Statement

Inclusion in US museums gained momentum in 2014 when AAM released its first inclusion-related document, a *Diversity and Inclusion Policy Statement*. This policy statement built on the Alliance's previous efforts centered on the realities of museums in a pluralistic, multicultural society with the publication of *Excellence and Equity* (1992) and the toolkit *Mastering Civic Engagement* (2002). The 2014 *Diversity and Inclusion Policy Statement*, however, was the first to explicitly focus on the language of inclusion.

i. Background and Development

Beginning in 2014, the AAM engaged in a couple of concerted efforts to develop a definition of inclusion for the field. These efforts had two main objectives: (1) to make the organizational culture of AAM more inclusive and (2) to set the tone for the museum field through the formulation of standards and best practices that center on inclusion.

In 2014, AAM recognized that its membership was not carrying out diversity and inclusion goals as comprehensively as it would have liked. Additionally, AAM recognized it needed to make internal changes as well. In response, the AAM's board formed a task force centered on diversity and inclusion with the mission to formulate a policy statement that would clarify what diversity and inclusion means conceptually and in practice for the Alliance and the field (Harris and Staveloz, 2014).[5]

According to the AAM, the policy statement's focus areas were human capital, key stakeholders, and products and resources. It aimed to create change on two levels. The first was internal to the operations of the Alliance. For instance, when the policy was released in 2014, it was incorporated into AAM's Operational Plan, where it affected hiring, promotion, and other facets of the organization. It also shifted the focus of the Alliance's online Information Center to include more resources on diversity and inclusion for its members. The second level of impact was focused externally toward the Alliance's membership. Namely, AAM set the intention to make revisions to its museum accreditation expectations to center diversity and inclusion (Harris and Staveloz, 2014). This level of impact is still developing. In 2019, the Alliance launched the *Facing Change* initiative and established a task force to develop recommendations to embed diversity, equity, accessibility, and inclusion more significantly into its excellence programs, including accreditation (AAM, 2018).[6]

In the AAM's 2014 policy statement, the task force defined inclusion as follows:

> The act of including; a strategy to leverage diversity. Diversity always exists in social systems. Inclusion, on the other hand, must be created. In order to leverage diversity, an environment must be created where people feel supported, listened to, and able to do their personal best.

In contrast to the United Kingdom, where the museum field was linked to inclusion-specific governmental mandates, the US museum field was required to craft its understanding of inclusion outside of a comprehensive national framework. As such, AAM turned to the business world to formulate its stance on inclusion.[7] Indeed, by 2014, it had become increasingly common for big businesses, such as Nike and Coca-Cola, to develop diversity and inclusion statements.

In its statement, the Alliance framed diversity as an institutional asset to be leveraged through inclusion, that is, through the creation of an environment where people can feel supported to achieve their personal best (Harris and Staveloz, 2014). This approach to formulating diversity as an asset to be leveraged is known as the *business case* for diversity and inclusion. The business case for diversity and inclusion holds that leveraging and shifting the internal demographic makeup of an organization, in other words, its diversity, can lead to outputs that will better represent and appeal to a broader base (Hyter and Turnock, 2006). In the business world, this case for diversity and inclusion is presented as a means for increased profits to an organization's bottom line.

The Incluseum was the first venue to publicly publish AAM's *Diversity and Inclusion Policy Statement*, which had only been released internally up until that point.[8] We aimed to bring this statement within *The Incluseum*'s dialogic space and collaboratively inquire about it. How did the perspective promoted in the statement fit within the ongoing dialogue on inclusion in museums? Did the community of practitioners and scholars invested in this conversation find it satisfactory? How could this work be built on? Moreover, AAM's Diversity Committee (DivCom), a professional committee of the Alliance, organized several actions centered on bringing the policy to the Alliance's members. For example, in April 2015, DivCom organized a live, online question-and-answer session between AAM members and AAM leaders who chaired the diversity and inclusion task force. DivCom's goal was to generate bottom-up engagement with a policy that had been generated in a top-down manner.

ii. Criticism

The position of the policy as a business case created tension in the field. To many, it seemed that framing the goal of diversity and inclusion as a business case confused its intentions. Indeed, instead of either being about addressing legacies of exclusion or better fulfilling museums' public responsibilities and aspirations, the business case seemed to reduce inclusion as a way to contribute to an institution's financial bottom line. Reflecting this tension, Porchia Moore explained her reservations about AAM's decision to frame diversity as an asset, stating, "The truth is that I do not like the term 'diversity' because I find it to be a racially coded term which exacts all sorts of confusing sentimentalities and hidden agendas" (Moore, 2014). Moore's perspective is in line with critical race scholars who, like Susan VanDeventer Iverson (2007), warned that without criticality about power, diversity and inclusion discourses run the risk of reducing people of color to commodities that organizations can strategically utilize to "acquire or maintain a competitive edge in the market" (p. 600). Nancy Leong (2013) coined this problematic practice "racial capitalism," or "the process of deriving social and economic value from the racial identity of another person" (p. 2153).

These critical voices extend beyond the museum field and are part of a larger chorus that has encouraged greater critical reflection in how the term "inclusion" is used. Many have noted that the positive valence ascribed to inclusion tends to obscure how dynamics of power and oppression structure social group differences, or diversity, hampering the ability to question how these structures operate within an organization and society at large (Ahmed, 2012; Gotsis and Kortezi, 2015; Grimes, 2002; Herring and Henderson, 2012). How did AAM take this into consideration? How would it ensure that its approach to diversity and inclusion reached beyond a surface-level position and would instead be rooted in a critical yet generative understanding of the ways in which inclusion is tethered to social justice (Deem and Ozga, 2020; Paquet Kinsley, 2016)? These questions, among others, reverberated in the US museum field in the years following AAM's release of its policy statement.

b) AAM's 2018 Diversity, Equity, Accessibility, and Inclusion Report

Reflecting the ongoing, field-wide momentum to center inclusion as a key value for the sector, AAM continued its efforts to refine its understanding of inclusion and bring this value to the core of its operations. Beginning in 2015, the Alliance engaged in dialogue with thought leaders, practitioners, and activists organizing for greater inclusion in museums in view of formulating diversity and inclusion as crucially important areas of focus for the field. Specifically, the Alliance's strategic plan for 2016–2020 stated that it would focus on "diversity, equity, accessibility and inclusion in all aspects of museum structure and programming," identifying this topic as one that the Alliance's membership "strongly believes to be vital to the future viability, relevance and sustainability of museums" (AAM, n.d.).

In 2018, the AAM gathered a working group to explore inclusion within the greater context of diversity, equity, and accessibility (DEAI). The working group was made up of twenty museum professionals, representing a variety of disciplines, organizational sizes and types, and perspectives. Together, the group produced a report titled *Facing Change: Insights from AAM's DEAI Working Group*. This report addressed some of the criticism discussed earlier pertaining to AAM's 2014 *Diversity and Inclusion Policy Statement*. In this report, inclusion is no longer framed as a mere business case, but understood in relation to equity, an approach more rooted in social justice which recognizes that genuine inclusion requires that past exclusions be acknowledged and fairly and justly remediated (AAM, 2018).

The report opens with a statement from AAM's now former director of inclusion Nicole Ivy, who places inclusion within the context of historical inequalities that have shaped the field, echoing the earlier discussion of the New Museology and the need to contend with systemic exclusion in museums. Furthermore, she calls out the problematic labor practices that have made it difficult for people of low income and racially minoritized groups to have access to museum employment opportunities. Situating inclusion in such a way brings it within a reflexive frame, addressing the critics and limitations of inclusion as a business case.

The potential reflexive nature of inclusion is further emphasized in Ivy's opening words to the *Facing Change* report. She says,

> The work [of inclusion] doesn't begin "out there," in some space external to museum staff, directors, and boards. Nor does it hinge solely on outreach to underserved populations. Effective inclusion work begins inside the structures of our museums and within each of us. (AAM, 2018, p. 2)

Her focus on the structural/institutional and individual changes that inclusion work calls for echoes the perspective that Chris Taylor (2016), former founding director of inclusion and community engagement at the Minnesota Historical Society, presented on the AAM's Center for the Future of Museums (CFM) blog. He explains that museums typically "Do Diversity" through programming aimed at audiences from diverse communities. Many of these programs—though engaging—are created in Euro-centric organizations by staff who seldom represent the target community. *Systemic inclusion* calls for museums to look internally at their processes, procedures, policies and the cultural competence of staff. (emphasis added)

Both of these statements emphasize the reflexive nature of inclusion work and the need for it to be systemic; inclusion requires that the internal structures of museums, their processes, procedures, and policies, be examined and transformed.

Moreover, the reflexivity Ivy and Taylor both speak of encompasses the self, or individual staff members' competence for the work. This final point is important as it stresses the fact that genuine inclusion requires more than new internal processes, procedures, and policies; it implicates the self and requires a willingness to see reflexively the noninnocent and nonneutral realities of our embodied subjectivities.

The AAM *Facing Change* working group developed five insights that structure the report and contextualize inclusion work:

1. Every museum professional must do personal work to face their unconscious bias;
2. Debate on definitions must not hinder progress;
3. Inclusion is central to the effectiveness and sustainability of museums;
4. Systemic change is vital to long-term, genuine progress;
5. Empowered, inclusive leadership is essential at all levels of an organization. (AAM, 2018, p. 4)

These five insights constitute a greater context that inclusion is placed within, making clear that the pursuit of inclusion is fundamental to museums' sustainability. Again, self-reflexivity (examining unconscious bias) is emphasized as a central practice. Moreover, systemic change is underlined as vital. Finally, supportive leadership is also stressed as being at the core of inclusion work, an insight that AAM is now building upon with its *Facing Change: Advancing Museum Board Diversity and Inclusion* initiative. Taken together, these insights highlight how AAM is shaping an understanding of inclusion for the field in a way that focuses on individual and institutional/ structural work to shift museums' work culture and practices. This internal work is prioritized as key to generating inclusive relationships with audiences and creating inclusive programs.

Within this greater context, AAM further describes the distinction between inclusion and diversity, defining inclusion as follows:

The intentional, ongoing effort to ensure that diverse individuals fully participate in all aspects of organizational work, including decision-making processes. It also refers to the ways that diverse participants are valued as respected members of an organization and/or community. While a truly "inclusive" group is necessarily diverse, a "diverse" group may or may not be "inclusive." (2018, p. 8)

Inclusion, from this perspective, factors into a museum's managerial strategy rather than only being a guide for the development of products and services. Specifically, this definition focuses on the intentional and ongoing nature of creating inclusion as a focus of an organization's culture.

In comparison to AAM's 2014 formulation of inclusion, this definition no longer describes inclusion as "a strategy to leverage diversity." This indicates an evolution from primarily framing diversity and inclusion as a business case, and thus a move away from the problematic connotation of racial capitalism evoked by that framing. Moreover, it is important to note that the 2018 formulation of inclusion represents a polyvocal process. The AAM was upfront about who participated in the process of developing these definitions and what the process entailed. This matters because it demonstrates greater transparency and accountability to the field.

c) Beyond AAM: Voices from the Field

While AAM was working toward defining inclusion and related concepts between 2014 and 2018, widespread dialogue and action was also occurring in the field about what genuine inclusion entails. This dialogue was characterized by museum professionals leveraging social media such as blog platforms and Twitter to connect, share ideas, and organize in a grassroots and activist fashion to learn together and have their voices heard (Coleman and Moore, 2019). Examples of such digitally mediated dialogue and social organizing includes *The Incluseum*, #MuseumsRespondToFerguson (#MRTF, whose leadership is discussed in the next section), Museum Hue (founded and directed by Stephanie A. Johnson-Cunningham and Monica O. Montgomery), Museum of Impact (also founded by Monica O. Montgomery), #MuseumWorkersSpeak (#MWS, whose founders are discussed in the next section), #museumsarenotneutral (founded by La Tanya Autry and Mike Murawski), Visitors of Color (founded by nikhil trivedi and Porchia Moore), and the Empathetic Museum (founded by Gretchen Jennings, with current members also including Janeen Bryant, Stacey Mann, Kayleigh Bryant-Greenwell, Jim Cullen, Charlette Hove, Jackie Peterson, Nayeli Zepeda, and Ryan Hill).[9] Many of these movements quickly grew to include more people and have had evolving leadership cohorts. While not fully digitally mediated, another noteworthy collaborative and impactful action that took place during this time frame is Museum As Site for Social Action (MASS Action).[10] FWD: Museums Journal, based within the museum and exhibition studies program at the University of Illinois at Chicago directed by Therese Quinn, was also a unique project that came about in these years and put graduate students at the center of editorial decisions about publishing content emphasizing vanguard and social justice–oriented approaches to museum work. Taken together, these initiatives form a network we call the Inclusive Museum Movement (Moore, 2016), all of which emerged during a unique moment of insurgency (Quinn, 2016).

We now focus on three of these initiatives, namely, #MRTF, #MWS, and MASS Action, to highlight their contributions to the ongoing meaning making and dialogue on inclusion in museums.

i. Museums Respond to Ferguson (#MRTF)

#MRTF emerged in December 2014 as a response to the numerous recent acts of unprosecuted police violence against people of color and the overall lack of responsiveness from the museum sector (Jennings, 2015).[11] Initiated by museum practitioner and consultant Gretchen Jennings, a group of museum and arts bloggers coordinated digitally on drafting a joint statement urging US museums that purport to care about inclusion to respond to events like the ones that took place in Ferguson, Missouri, in 2014. During this time of escalating outcry about police brutality and unnecessary use of force targeting Black people, many asked: Are we at a turning point for discussions about race in the United States? And by extension, a turning point in our museums that desire to be inclusive, function as a forum, and be relevant to local communities they are situated within? Each blogger then released the statement on their respective platforms.[12]

This statement spurred an ongoing professional dialogue in the US museum field that led to several online and offline actions that continue to have ripple effects to this day. Most immediately following the publication of the statement in December 2014, a group of museum practitioners and scholars led by Adrianne Russell and Aleia Brown hosted monthly Tweetchats using the hashtag #MuseumsRespondToFerguson.[13] These chats offered museum professionals from all over the country a chance to join the conversation on race/racism and its intersections (that is, other systems of oppression such as gender, class, and sexual preferences) in museums, responding to current events in our communities, and continuous issues of inclusion in cultural spaces (Fletcher, 2016; Jennings, 2015). Two characteristics of these chats are that many of the discussions centered on the "continued lack of progress in diversifying boards, professional staff, and volunteer corps in museums" (Jennings, 2015) and that they relied on a diverse group of museum professionals, particularly younger individuals (Jennings, 2015).

In May 2015, another action that arose from #MRTF was the formation of the group Museums and Race. This group was initially convened during the 2015 AAM Annual Meeting in Atlanta, Georgia, and was facilitated by members of The Museum Group (TMG).[14] This initial action is the seed that has grown into an ongoing movement called Museums and Race: Transformation and Justice, which aims to challenge and reimagine institutional policies and systems that perpetuate oppressions in museums. Museums and Race organized museum professionals through, for example, a gathering of museum practitioners and thinkers in Chicago in 2016 as well as events and unconferences that have taken place in conjunction with the AAM annual conferences every year since.[15] Two of the twenty-four participants at the 2016 Museums and Race Chicago gathering who have continued to lead on the project's steering committee since that time are Omar Eaton-Martinez and Janeen Bryant.

Overall, the #MRTF statement and its ensuing activities helped create a tighter knit community of practitioners and scholars, helping them "understand that they are not alone in their pursuit towards more inclusive spaces," especially in a context where "several museums gave official directives to personnel not to discuss Ferguson or any of the other related incidents" (Fletcher, 2016). Today, these practitioners and scholars who center equity, accessibility, diversity, and inclusion in their work continue to work together. Examples of collaboration include special topic publications,[16] conference workshops and presentations, *The Incluseum* blogposts, and large-scale collaborative projects such as Museum as Site for Social Action (MASS Action), which we come back to shortly.[17]

#MRTF brought forth two aspects of what authentic inclusion entails. The first centers on the need for greater understanding of how racism has operated—and continues to operate—in museum spaces and in museums' relationships with their local communities. As Gretchen Jennings (2015) states, "Ferguson in its broader sense has given the field an opportunity, and a kind of permission, to raise the specific issues of race, racism, and white privilege in the context of museums in a way that has not happened before" (p. 101). The second element of inclusion that #MRTF illuminated is the responsibility of museums to respond to issues that are affecting the country and the local communities in which they are situated and that they purport to serve. Museums do not exist in a vacuum, and they are not neutral spaces; inclusion is about relationships.

ii. Museum Workers Speak (#MWS)

Another activist movement that brought insight into what genuine inclusion entails is #MWS, "an action-oriented platform for social change at the intersection of labor, access, and inclusion" (Museum Workers Speak, n.d.) that organized emerging museum professionals, graduate students, and museum staff members. #MWS arose in 2015 with a "rogue session" at AAM's 2015 conference in Atlanta. This gathering highlighted a couple of important facets of shifting toward more inclusion in museums. The first was how internal museum practices including hiring, leadership, and work environment present barriers to entry and advancement rooted in race and class. One of #MWS's focal points was the common museum practice of unpaid internships, which are often required for entry into the field. Given their unpaid status, these internships privilege those who can afford unremunerated labor, thus directly undermining the diversity among museum staff (Walker, 2019, p. 125). The second facet was the intersectional nature of labor practices in museums. In the words of #MWS cofounders Alyssa Greenberg and Nina Pelaez (2015),

> A discussion about museum labor practices is inevitably a discussion about racism, sexism, misogyny, elitism, and various other social inequalities. We found that by speaking openly about labor, we opened the door to frank conversations about race and privilege that might not otherwise have gotten off the ground.

#MWS was truly a grassroots movement facilitated "by a diverse team of emerging museum professionals [who are] uniquely aware of the challenges presented by working in this field" (Greenberg and Pelaez, 2015). The group hosted a Tweetchat every month for a year and organized regional groups for face-to-face gatherings in six US cities. Moreover, members of #MWS participated in several conferences between 2015 and 2016 and put pressure on AAM to center internal labor practices in its inclusion-related efforts, which was reflected in its 2018 *Facing Change* report discussed earlier. Through this activism, internal inequities related to labor practices were brought to the forefront of dialogues on inclusion in the field.

FIGURE 1.1
MWS flyer distributed at the 2015 AAM Conference in Atlanta announcing a "rogue session" held at a local art gallery to discuss employment issues in museums.
Design by Jillian Reese

iii. Museum As Site for Social Action (MASS Action)

Inspired by the calls to action of #MRTF and #MWS, MASS Action was a three-year collaborative project that launched in 2015, centering on the question: How do you transform museums from the inside out and align them with more equitable and inclusive practices? The project emerged when Elisabeth Callihan, former head of multigenerational learning at the Minneapolis Institute of Art and cofounder and project manager for MASS Action, reached out to and invited five museum professionals and scholars "who were asking questions and challenging the field" (Callihan, 2018) to act as advisors.[18] Together, they created a road map, "a plan for collaborative action that would be a call for greater equity and social justice in museums" (2018). Specifically, this road map outlined a three-year plan that would entail the cocreation of a tool kit (year 1) followed by its dissemination (year 2) and application (year 3).

The cocreation of the tool kit in year 1 represents a remarkable collaborative and multivocal process through which fifty-five museum "change-makers and thought-leaders" were identified and brought together (Callihan, 2018). This group gathered in person in Minneapolis in the fall of 2016 for an action-oriented conversation around topics of equity in museums, relevant programming, and community engagement. In addition to Elisabeth Callihan, Anniessa Antar and Amy Batiste took on crucial roles in MASS Action's evolution during this period.[19] Participants worked collaboratively to identify the most pressing issues in the field (MASS Action, n.d.). As Callihan recounts,

> For three days, we discussed the issues of institutional transformation, creating an inclusive culture, widening interpretation, sharing authority, decolonizing collections and the museum. We formed small working groups around these topics and began outlining our vision for a "tool kit."

The resulting tool kit includes eight coauthored essays that focus on the topics mentioned in the previous quote. These represent a guide to the emerging lexicon around equity and inclusion, some strategies to address inequity, along with seven accompanying worksheets to foster the development of more inclusive museums practices and a few other "tools" such as key terms and a DEAI staff engagement survey from the Minnesota Historical Society.

FIGURE 1.2
MASS Action Logo

In year 2, a larger convening was held to include staff teams from thirty museums that intended to use the tool kit and were committed to embedding strategies of inclusion into their institutions. The convening featured case studies, peer-to-peer learning opportunities, and other discussions of how to put theory into practice. This momentum was carried forward in year 3 when staff teams from sixty-four participating museums gathered to build upon the commitments to equity and social change agreed upon at the 2017 Convening (year 2), creating more inclusive practices in their own institutions and the field at large.

In sum, through the cocreation of the tool kit and a public convening, the intentions of MASS Action were to gather and share strategies and frameworks needed to align museums with more equitable and inclusive practices as well as build a network of practitioners and thinkers committed to this work. In the words of Callihan (2018):

> *MASS Action* is not a project anymore. It is a network of people, individuals committed to seeing the museum field change, connecting in solidarity, recognizing there is strength in numbers. That, like fractals, if we all individually commit to do our part on a small scale, we will start to see change on a large scale. That with enough voices, we can make change.

Beyond the three-year plan, MASS Action has maintained momentum and continued to organize museum professionals through the MASS Action Community of Practice and MASS Action Accountability Project, both of which place an emphasis on antiracism work in museums (more on this in chapter 4).[20]

The three projects presented here, and the many others mentioned in the opening paragraph of this section, represent a collective of museum workers, individuals personally motivated to organize because of their desire to change the field. These projects were unprecedented and groundbreaking in their ability to mobilize museum professionals at the grassroots level to demand a more capacious and justice-centered approach to inclusion in museums. They did so through providing pushback to top-down approaches to institutionalizing inclusion, mobilizing peers, promoting dialogue and horizontal organizational structures, as well as leveraging digital technologies to connect and amplify people and messages. These projects continue to have a significant impact in the field through the network of museum professionals they have woven and the outputs this network continues to generate. Taken together, these projects provide ongoing pushback, depth, and accountability to discourses of inclusion and DEIA in the field.

Finally, it is important to note that the list of projects, initiatives, and collective of individuals invested in this work has continued to grow since 2018. Examples of these include OF/BY/FOR/ALL, Death to Museums, and Change the Museum.[21] There have also been notable shifts in project activities, such as #MWS organizing mutual aid relief in support of museum workers laid off during the COVID-19 2020 pandemic, something we come back to in chapter 4. This widening web of projects continues to expand the field's understanding of inclusion.

Concurrent to the more project-oriented work described here, there have also been numerous individuals who have made distinct and significant contributions to the US museums field's understanding of inclusion.

The Importance of Understanding Where We Come From

Tracing the precursors of how inclusion is understood in museums today illu-minates a conceptual genealogy, mapping the relationships of individual and group-authored ideas that have shaped our understandings of inclusion over time. For those working in the museum field today, we inevitably encounter ideas about inclusion intersecting with our practice. We are better prepared to assess existing and new approaches to inclusion, or consider how they should inform our practice, when *we know where and from whom they come from*. This awareness additionally supports the field's ability to accurately acknowledge intellectual contributions. Our dominant, White supremacist culture manifests itself in the resistant, and sometimes reactionary, character of museum responses to new critiques. This can distract from and erase the contributions of those authoring and advocating for new approaches to inclu-sion, most commonly BIPOC authors and authors from historically margin-alized backgrounds and identities. This chapter is intended to interrupt the forgetting of where the US museum field has come from regarding inclusion in museums and the initiatives and voices that have shaped these conversa-tions along the way over the past decade.

Inclusion is a developing discourse, descended from, and related to, many connected efforts over time.

In the next chapter, we will deepen our discussion of the development of the concept of inclusion in museums by discussing contextual limitations, appropriation in practices that maintain White supremacy, and other abuses of the term that reduce, instead of expand, inclusion's potentiality for our field's reimagining of itself from the ground up.

Key Questions

1. What are other important examples, events, people, or movements that have shaped the course of inclusion in museums?
2. Flex your visionary muscles: Where would you like to see this journey of expanding inclusion in museums go? How do we get there?

3. What are your personal and institutional histories? How could taking stock of these narratives empower you to implement transformation?

4. Where do you see yourself in this movement? What can you do to amplify your voice and choice for movement and community building?

5. Who can you connect with now to add on to the work that you have done and will continue to do?

Notes

1. See https://www.smithsonianmag.com/smithsonian-institution/fifty-years -ago-idea-museum-people-came-age-180973828/; http://www.thehundred-seven .org/museums.html; http://www.6floors.org/teaching/wp-content/uploads/2016/08/ Creating-a-Dialogic-Museum.pdf; https://www.osagenation-nsn.gov/museum.

2. This paradigm constitutes the Western museum field's historical legacy, remnants of which are still alive today.

3. Of course, the veil of neutrality wasn't once and for all pierced; debates about museum neutrality are ongoing. See #museumsarenotneutral.

4. Ecomuseums emerged in France in the early 1970s as a form of community-based museum focused on the preservation and celebration of local cultural heritage and reliant on the participation of local communities for all aspects of their activities.

5. Part of the process involved in developing this policy statement entailed researching other organizations' diversity and inclusion policies and assessing how other organizations beyond nonprofits and museums carry forward their diversity and inclusion programming and policies (Harris and Staveloz, 2014).

6. See https://www.aam-us.org/programs/facing-change1/the-excellence-in-deai -task-force/.

7. It should be noted that official documents that AAM released pertaining to this policy do not indicate who was part of the task force and what was the process they engaged in.

8. See https://incluseum.com/2014/08/25/aams-diversity-and-inclusion-policy -statement/.

9. See https://www.incluseum.com/; https://adriannerussell.wordpress.com/ museumsrespondtofergusonarchive/; https://www.museumhue.com/; https://sites .google.com/view/museumworkersspeak/; https://www.museumsarenotneutral .com/; https://visitorsofcolor.tumblr.com/; http://empatheticmuseum.weebly.com/.

10. https://www.museumaction.org/.

11. Specifically, the spark that brought about #MRTF was the acquittal of policeman Darren Wilson in the shooting of an unarmed Black young man of eighteen years old, Michael Brown (Rest in Power), in late November 2014 in Ferguson, Missouri.

12. See https://incluseum.com/2014/12/22/joint-statement-from-museum-bloggers -colleagues-on-ferguson-related-events/.

13. See https://twitter.com/hashtag/museumsrespondtoferguson?lang=en; https:// incluseum.com/2015/12/17/we-who-believe-in-freedom-cannot-rest/.

14. The urgency of this dialogue and the need for subsequent action was heightened with the murder of another unarmed Black man at the hands of police officers in Baltimore, Maryland, Freddie Gray (Rest in Power), as we were convening in Atlanta at the time.

15. See https://museumsandrace.org/.

16. See, for example, https://www.tandfonline.com/toc/rjme20/42/2.

17. See https://www.museumaction.org/.

18. This initial group was made of Adrianne Russell, Aletheia Wittman, Chris Taylor, Porchia Moore, and Rose Paquet.

19. By this stage in the project's development, Anniessa Antar had also become a critical MASS Action staff lead at Mia, and Dr. Amy Batiste, CEO of Creative Catalysts, Inc., was working with Mia to orchestrate MASS Action gatherings and tool kit–creation efforts.

20. See https://www.museumaction.org/massaction-blog/2020/8/31/from -statements-of-solidarity-to-transformative-action-amp-accountability.

21. See https://www.ofbyforall.org; https://deathtomuseums.com/; https://www .instagram.com/changethemuseum/?hl=en.

Bibliography

Ahmed, Sara. *On Being Included: Racism and Diversity in Institutional Life.* Durham, NC: Duke University Press, 2012.

American Alliance of Museums. *American Alliance of Museums 2016–2020 Strategic Plan.* N.d. https://www.aam.us.org/programs/about-aam/american-alliance-of -museums-strategic-plan.

———. *Excellence and Equity: Education and the Public Dimension of Museums.* 1992. http://ww2.aam-us.org/docs/default-source/resource-library/excellence-and -equity.pdf.

———. *Mastering Civic Engagement: A Challenge to Museums.* 2002.

———. *Facing Change: Insights from AAM's Diversity, Equity, Accessibility, and Inclusion Working Group.* 2018. https://www.aam-us.org/programs/diversity-equity -accessibility-and-inclusion/facing-change/.

Bennett, Tony. *The Birth of the Museum: History, Theory, Politics.* New York: Routledge, 1995.

Bourdieu, Pierre. *The Field of Cultural Production: Essays on Art and Literature.* New York: Columbia University Press, 1993.

Burns, Andrea. *From Storefront to Monument: Tracing the Public History of the Black Museum Movement.* Amherst: University of Massachusetts Press, 2013.

Callihan, Elisabeth. "An Introduction to the Mass Action Toolkit from the Co-Founder." *The Incluseum,* July 23, 2018. https://incluseum.com/2018/07/23/ an-introduction-to-the-mass-action-toolkit-from-the-co-founder/.

Clifford, James. *Routes: Travel and Translation in the Late Twentieth Century.* Boston, MA: Harvard University Press, 1997.

Coleman, Laura Edyth, and Porchia Moore. "From the Ground Up: Grassroots Social Justice Activism in American Museums." In *Museum Activism*, edited by Robert E. Janes and Richard Sandell, 91–103. New York: Routledge, 2019.

Deem, Rosemary, and Jenny Ozga. "Women Managing for Diversity in a Postmodern World." In *Feminist Critical Policy Analysis II*, 25–40. New York: Routledge, 2020.

Department of Culture, Media, and Sports. *Museums for the Many: Standards for Museums and Galleries to Use When Developing Access Policies.* London: DCMS, 1999.

———. *Centres for Social Change: Museums, Galleries and Archives for All.* London: DCMS, 2000a.

———. *The Learning Power of Museums: A Vision for Museum Education.* London: DCMS and Department for Education and Employment, 2000b.

———. *Understanding the Future: Museums and 21st Century.* London: DCMS, 2005.

Dodd, Jocelyn, and Richard Sandell. *Including Museums: Perspectives on Museums, Galleries and Social Inclusion.* Leicester: Research Center for Museums and Galleries, University of Leicester, 2001.

Fletcher, Kami. "#MuseumsRespondToFerguson: An Interview with Aleia Brown and Adrianne Russell." *Black Perspectives*, September 29, 2016. https://www.aaihs .org/museumsrespondtoferguson-an-interview-with-aleia-brown-and-adrianne -russell/.

Gotsis, George, and Zoe Kortezi. *Critical Studies in Diversity Management Literature: A Review and Synthesis*: Dordrecht: Springer. 2015.

Greenberg, Alyssa, and Nina Pelaez. "Unsafe Ideas: Building Museum Worker Solidarity for Social Justice." Center for the Future of Museums Blog, The American Alliance of Museums, June 2, 2015. https://www.aam-us.org/2015/06/02/unsafe -ideas-building-museum-worker-solidarity-for-social-justice/.

Grimes, Diane Susan. "Challenging the Status Quo? Whiteness in the Diversity Management Literature." *Management Communication Quarterly* 15, no. 3 (2002): 381–409.

Group for Large Local Authority Museums. *Museums and Social Inclusion: GLLAM Report.* Leicester: Research Center for Museums and Galleries, University of Leicester, 2000. https://www2.le.ac.uk/departments/museumstudies/rcmg/projects/ musms-and-social-inclusion-the-gllam-report/GLLAM%20Interior.pdf.

Harris, William, and Auntaneshia Staveloz. "AAM's Diversity and Inclusion Policy Statement Part I and II." *The Incluseum*, August 25, 2014. http://incluseum.com/ 2014/08/25/aams diversityandinclusion-policy-statement/.

Herring, Cedric, and Loren Henderson. "From Affirmative Action to Diversity: Toward a Critical Diversity Perspective." *Critical Sociology* 38, no. 5 (2012): 629–43.

Hooper-Greenhill, Eilean. *Museums and the Shaping of Knowledge.* New York: Routledge, 1992.

Hyter, Michael, and Judith Turnock. *The Power of Inclusion: Unlock the Potential and Productivity of Your Workplace.* Hoboken, NJ: John Wiley & Sons, 2006.

Iverson, Susan VanDeventer. "Camouflaging Power and Privilege: A Critical Race Analysis of University Diversity Policies." *Educational Administration Quarterly* 43, no. 5 (2007): 586–611.

Jennings, Gretchen. "The #museumsrespondtoFerguson Initiative, a Necessary Conversation." *Museums and Social Issues* 10, no. 2 (2015): 97–105.

Leong, Nancy. "Racial Capitalism." *Harvard Law Review* 126, no. 8 (2013): 2153–225. http://harvardlawreview.org/wpcontent/uploads/pdfs/vol126_leong.pdf.

Levitas, Ruth. "The Idea of Social Inclusion." Presentation to the CCSD/HRDC Social Inclusion Research Conference, Ottawa, March 27–28, 2003.

Macdonald, Sharon. "Introduction." In *A Companion to Museum Studies*, edited by Sharon Macdonald, 1–12. Oxford: Blackwell, 2006.

Mason, Rhiannon. "Cultural Theory and Museum Studies." In *A Companion to Museum Studies*, edited by Sharon Macdonald, 17–32. Oxford: Blackwell, 2006.

Moore, Porchia. "The Danger of the 'D' Word: Museums and Diversity." *The Incluseum*, January 20, 2014. https://incluseum.com/2014/01/20/the-danger-of-the-d-word-museums-and-diversity/.

———. "The Inclusive Museum Movement." *Museum*, November/December 2016.

Museum as Sites for Social Action. N.d. https://www.museumaction.org/about.

Museum Workers Speak. N.d. https://museumworkersspeak.weebly.com/.

Paquet Kinsley, Rose. "Inclusion in Museums: A Matter of Social Justice." *Museums, Management, and Curatorship* 31, no. 5 (2016): 474–90.

Patterson, Adam, Aletheia Wittman, Chieko Phillips, Gamynne Guillotte, Therese Quinn, and Adrianne Russell. "Getting Started: What We Need to Change and Why." *Museum as Site for Social Action Toolkit.* 2017. https://www.museumaction.org/resources/.

Quinn, Therese. "Welcome." Issue #1 Inaugurations. FWD: Museums Journal, 2016.

Sandell, Richard. "Museums as Agents of Social Inclusion." *Museum Management and Curatorship* 17, no. 4 (1998): 401–418.

———. "Museums and the Combating of Social Inequality." In *Museums, Society, Inequality*, edited by Richard Sandell, 3–23. New York: Routledge, 2002.

———. "Social Inclusion, the Museum and the Dynamics of Sectorial Change." *Museum and Society* 1, no. 1 (2003): 45–62.

———. *Museums, Prejudice and the Reframing of Difference.* New York: Routledge, 2007.

Sandell, Richard, and Eithne Nightingale. *Museums, Equality and Social Justice.* New York: Routledge, 2013.

Shellman, Cecile. "Museum Musings: Inclusion Then and Now." In *Diversity, Equity, Accessibility, and Inclusion in Museums*, edited by Johnetta Betsch Cole and Laura L. Lott, 121–26. Lanham, MD: Rowman & Littlefield, 2019.

Taylor, Chris. "Doing Diversity in Museums." The Center for the Future of Museums Blog, The American Alliance of Museums, February 25, 2016. https://www.aam-us.org/2016/02/25/do-ing-diversity in-museums/.

Tlili, Anwar. "Efficiency and Social Inclusion: Implications for the Museum Profession." *Cadernos de Sociomuseologia* 43 (2012): 5–34.

Tlili, Anwar, Sharon Gewirtz, and Alan Cribb. "New Labour's Socially Responsible Museum: Roles, Functions and Greater Expectations." *Policy Studies* 28, no. 3 (2007): 269–89.

Vergo, Peter. "Introduction." In *The New Museology*, edited by Peter Vergo, 1–4. London: Reaktion Books, 1989.

Walker, Darren. "Twin Threats: How Ignorance and Instrumentality Create Inequality and Injustice." In *Diversity, Equity, Accessibility, and Inclusion in Museums*, edited by Johnetta Betsch Cole and Laura L. Lott, 121–26. Lanham, MD: Rowman & Littlefield, 2019.

Weil, Stephen. "From Being about Something to Being for Somebody: The Ongoing Transformation of the American Museum." *Daedalus* 128, no. 3 (1999): 229–58.

2

On the Limits of Inclusion

The Limits of Imagination

JUST AS IN MATHEMATICS, understanding the limits of a term is necessary for proper analysis of its value. If in the museum field we are concerned about the value of inclusion, then we are equally required to explicate the limits of that value as a concept. Inclusion is a concept accepted within the worldview of cultural heritage museum professionals who examine the nature of all of our work through the lens of diversity, equity, access, inclusion, belonging, decolonization, and/or social justice. It is a concept that advocates there is "goodness" or "qualities of efficacy" that enhance our work and standing as a profession that can be communicated to our communities, visitors, and ourselves as practitioners. We accept the universality of a need for its presence. And yet even if all of us agree upon instituting the values, practices, and discourse associated with inclusion, inclusion is not a plan of action. And action requires the infinite possibilities of imagination to construct viable plans.

Therefore, one of the first limits of inclusion is that how it is understood as both value and concept is susceptible to the limits of one's imagination and subsequently the collective imagination of institutional leadership. It is not a given that behind the closed doors of one's home, each museum professional holds the values of IEAJ as integral or important to their own lives or that they are practicing these values at the level of the personal. This is an important distinction because the work of IEAJ is one of transformation and change on the institutional level as well as the personal one. Transformation and change is a course corrective from a previous or current standard that signals deficiencies. Social justice activist Grace Lee Boggs informs us that "you cannot change any society unless you take responsibility for it, unless you see yourself as belonging to it and responsible for changing it."[1] Museums are institutions but they are composed of individuals. While all of us benefit from varying degrees of privileges from within a continuum of identities and experiences, unless one has experienced living at the margins of the margins of the marginalized and oppressed it might prove difficult to imagine the totality of why inclusion matters even when guided by the wisdom of empathy.

As such, inclusion as a value is in tension with the limits of imagination. Inclusion as an ideology can be embraced as an intellectual exercise while simultaneously being aggravated by the demands of real life decision making, which should be steered by core values. The values associated with IEAJ are often complex, emotionally heavy, politically charged, and filled with nuance. In these cases, the existence of black and white binaries of choice are removed and decision making lies within shades of gray. It is the values of IEAJ that are core or central to decision making that announce the true commitment to inclusive vision, and this requires imagination—the shaping of a new reality. For instance, when a global pandemic such as the coronavirus threatens the continuity of service and mandated quarantine demands that museums close their doors to the public, museum leaders would activate the core values of IEAJ and work to keep their employees employed and financially solvent as opposed to being at the mercy of navigating unemployment and uncertain futures due to mass firings and furloughs. The financial bottom line does not supersede a core value of treating staff in such a way; equity and justice set a precedent for care and empathy during a collective global traumatic event. Imagination is the creative fluidity that helps us move from current reality to world-building potentials that rest on shaping new structures of meaning.

Inclusion remains a viable option because it is wrought with possibility, and possibility is based on the infinite wisdom of imagination. The limits, then, are bound only by the lack of imagination of individuals. Perhaps this is why collective imagining, a kind of dreaming by the collective, is necessary. In his germinal work *Freedom Dreams: The Black Radical Imagination,* Robin D. G. Kelley (2002) suggests that there is power in imagining as a collective:

> Without new visions, we don't know what to build, only what to knock down. We not only end up confused, rudderless and cynical, but we forget that making a revolution is not a series of clever maneuvers and tactics, but a process that can and must transform us.

If inclusion is being institutionalized, what are the ways in which a collective vision can be dimmed by the limited imagining of the individual? Kelley's reminder is especially poignant when compared with the activism and legacy of Martin Luther King Jr., whose dream has been canonized to represent the challenges of overhauling systemic and institutional oppressions over time as imagining through dreaming. Inclusion is a valued framework in our field that becomes compromised when what IEAJ looks like and can mean in museums is limited by lack of imagination.

In her groundbreaking book *Emergent Strategy: Shaping Change, Changing Worlds*, adrienne maree brown illuminates the limits of imagination:

> We are in an imagination battle.
>
> Trayvon Martin and Mike Brown and Renisha McBride and so many others are dead because, in some white imagination, they were dangerous. And that imagination is so respected that those who kill, based on an imagined, radical-ized fear of Black people, are rarely held accountable. Imagination has people thinking they can go from being poor to a millionaire as part of a shared American dream. Imagination turns Brown bombers into terrorists and white bombers into mentally ill victims. Imagination gives us borders, gives us superiority, gives us race as an indicator of ability. I often feel I am trapped inside someone else's imagination, and I must engage my own imagination in order to break free. (2017, p. 18)

Liberating museums from the tyranny of institutional, systemic, and cultural racism is predicated upon imagining new ways of being the institution that we know of called "museums." It requires leaning in toward the possibilities of shaping a new organism. This is at the heart of the origins of *The Incluseum* project.

One museum executive director imagines that the work of IEAJ means that extending the museum hours from 5 p.m. nightly to 8 p.m. is the best way to increase visitor engagement, while another imagines that the language of inclusion means that all text panels in an exhibition include English, Spanish, and Arabic to reflect the multilingual needs of their specific community. One museum education professional imagines the work of IEAJ means that outreach is composed of targeting Latinx communities, while another imagines that creating a program to support veterans is the most effective means of interacting with an older visitor demographic. None of these visions are wrong or incorrect. In fact, they might all prove effective. Yet they are still limited in scope by an imagination informed by decades of genealogical ideology passed down by scholars and practitioners nourished by the rhetoric of *diversity*.

The Hegemony of Diversity Discourse

It is critical to unpack the discourse of diversity in museums as one of the most critical limits of inclusion. Historically, the lexicon included specific vocabulary that referenced a visual embodiment of what the museum field and museums should look like. Terms such as multicultural, multiethnic, multinational, cross-culturalism, and pluralism all echoed a desire for museums to be diverse. Diversity is a term often used in the awareness that there are gaping racial disparities within museums. *It is employed as a tactic with the expected outcome of rectifying these disparities by actively seeking out and incorporating excluded members to join in an established organized system* (see also chapter 1). Within the context of museums, the discourse of inclusion is often used as a tactic in response to criticism that museums' workforce, public programming, collections, and exhibitions are not "diverse." In this manner, "diversity initiatives" are employed largely to dispel a notion of contrition toward cultural hierarchies of power where White ways of knowing are reflected dominantly in a museum's culture.

The error in a discourse of diversity is that patterns of exclusion are only interrupted temporarily and firm organizational structures remain intact. Discourses of diversity only do well to further secure and promote the notion that participation for visitors of color are relegated to acts of invitation. When museums seek diversity as a tool for including historically disengaged visitors, it becomes unclear who benefits from inclusion. In this sense, the ideological approach to attempting to be racially inclusive becomes a moot action because people of color remain powerless to change social structures pervasive in how the museum operates. In particular, this ideological approach of diversity does not recognize structural racism but merely attempts to keep the status quo intact while implementing change in increments of which no genuine transformation can be detected. The participation of visitors of color at this level of inclusion essentially diminishes them to the role of actors who provide a diverse experience for the museum as an institution and more importantly provides a racially diverse experience for the predominately White visitor. To this end, diversity as an inclusive ideology only gives the appearance of inclusion without actually going on to provide an equally diverse experience of racial inclusivity for the visitor of color. Furthermore, diversity initiatives usually originate from within the museum. This is again problematic because visitors of color have no input on the crafting of these initiatives and documents. Therefore when museums craft diversity initiatives on their own without the express input from visitors of color, it hinders any genuine opportunities for inclusion in the following ways:

1. Visitors of color are unable to clearly provide the racial labels for how they want to be identified.
2. Museums continue to take agency over their institutions as sources of power.
3. Visitors of color remain powerless to heavily influence their interests and tastes in relation to public programs, curatorial collection practices, exhibitions, etc.
4. Value is placed on the museum as *institution* with minimal value on the impact that *inclusion* might have on the visitors' of color communities—in this sense the efficacy of inclusion is unknown.
5. Diversity statements written by museum professionals make the assumptions that they know what visitors want or need.
6. Continues to silence the voice of the marginalized visitor.
7. Diversity statements in general are vague statements that fail to embed action in a responsive way with procedures in place to hold the museum accountable for a failure to implement these changes as perceived by the community.

In truth, the dogma of diversity speaks to a particular kind of color-coded visual optics regarding racial representation of personnel and visitorship. These initiatives do not necessarily enforce the kind of harmful philosophies of colorblindness but do suggest a kind of desire for assimilation. The vocabulary can be reduced to a quantitative metric of "inclusion." We can visually "see" the diversity as represented by the quantity of "X" demographic. Note as well that discourses of inclusion within the museum field have been predicated on the notion that there is a void or absence of "The Other" among the backdrop of the established or normative: those who "Belong." In other words, for predominately White-facing institutions, discourses of diversity and inclusion are overwhelmingly about being able to rely upon the metrics of "The Other." In fact, when diversity is aligned with quantifying racial and ethnic identity without specifically calling out and naming race, this highlights the critical limits of diversity discourse as it fails to identify the root cause of the lack of representation—racism itself. This failure to name institutional, cultural, and systemic racism indicates a longtime problem with the way that museums have danced around the issue of diversity and inclusion. Conflating issues of diversity as speaking to all of the "-isms" without truly addressing issues of race complicates the issue rather than explicating or offering solutions. It is also a failure to demonstrate the ways in which inclusion must be framed as in intersectional praxis and not singular strategic plans that function as if museum professionals and museum visitors are monolithic in their lived experiences. Discourses of diversity limit the possibilities of inclusion that have the ability to challenge negative perceptions of museums as elitist institutions and put in their stead fresh, new counter-narratives and historical perspectives.

Where for so long the term "diversity" in the museum field has been part of the lexicon alluding to the historic deficiencies of Black and BIPOC museum professionals, it referenced the low visitor engagement and participation rates of these demographics as well. As an afterthought additional marginalized groups would also be roughly hewn into this discourse. Diversity and then inclusion became a way to reference the people with disabilities, the economically challenged, queer, senior citizens, and any group whose representation was low or historically underengaged. As a result, this language represents a kind of code. The code alludes to "The Other" and the ways in which these groups did or did not adhere to behavioral or quantifiable standards of the "Belonged," the group whose ways of knowing, access to power, and cultural behaviors are viewed as the normative and accepted ways of being/visiting. This "signaled" to the "Belonged" that there needed to be a response or effort to "invite" this group to experience proximity to Whiteness and/or social and cultural power.

In more recent years, due to the collective labor of museum activists and scholars, inclusion has become synonymous with race and institutional racism in museums while simultaneously alluding to inclusion as a framework for addressing sexism, ableism, classism, equity, access, ageism, etc. Inclusion is a framework, but it cannot be a language coverall as it relates to issues of race. When we interrogate inclusion at the topic level—examining any range of topics from accessibility for physically challenged visitors to visitors on the autism spectrum, or from the lack of ethnically/racially diverse staff to low visitation of visitors of color, and to poor representation of diverse topics, artifacts, and exhibitions speaking to socioeconomic conditions—without truly unpacking racism, it renders institutional and systemic racism invisible. It also reduces the caustic impacts of racism and minimizes its harm, reach, and power.

The Architecture of Racism

The failure to center race and racism and the role that these two aspects play in the discourse of diversity and inclusion is a critical limit of inclusion work. As such, it becomes significantly important for museums and their professionals to understand why race matters. First Lady Michelle Obama alluded to similar sentiments in her 2015 opening remarks for the reopening of the Whitney Museum, stating, "There are so many kids in this country who look at places like museums and concert halls and other cultural centers, and they think to themselves, 'Well, that's not a place for me—for someone who looks like me, for someone who comes from my neighborhood."[2] Obama received a fair amount of criticism from a number of media outlets with her statement, with the *Washington Times* leading with an article titled "Michelle Obama Says Black Kids Feel Unwelcome at Museums; Cultural Institutions" (Chasmar, 2015).

Furthermore, the problem with the way that museums have addressed the issue of diversity and inclusion is that it has been framed in ways that do more to complicate than explicate or offer solutions. For example, museums tend to acknowledge that lack of representation is a problem but have difficulty looking within to hold themselves accountable for their role in how diversity and inclusion has been identified as something to achieve through initiatives rather than practiced values. As Sara Ahmed (2012) teaches us, race matters more than the hegemonic strategy of diversity, and inclusion cannot ever be successfully institutionalized. Diversity becomes what Ahmed calls "institutional performance." In her early essay "'You end up doing the document rather than doing the doing': Diversity, Race Equality and the Politics of Documentation," Ahmed (2007) points out that much emotional, intellectual, and physical labor is dedicated to performing the tasks of documenting goals for increasing diversity and inclusion without actually achieving inclusion. Thereby, efforts can be celebrated, evaluated, and laid bare as achievements without ever having to achieve anything. This is hegemony at its best—never having to change institutions. Institutional "best practices" remain firmly in place, and diversity is measured successfully by acquisition of quantifiable documents.

In terms of industry shifts influencing best practices, AAM's 2014 "Diversity and Inclusion" policy marks a transition in awareness for new methods of praxis; the definitions themselves were a guidepost for new praxis but did not provide new meanings for the subject of diversity and inclusion within the context of museums as central to the work of dismantling racism (see also chapter 1). Projects such as MASS Action, Museums and Race, The Visitors of Color Project, The Empathetic Museum, #MuseumsRespondToFerguson, Museums Are Not Neutral, Of/By/For/All, and others do well to advance the cause for centering race and racism. In short, AAM provides definitions that are general and not specific to achieving the action of these two concepts.

Discussions regarding diversity within museums tend to begin with analyzing Stephen Weil's 1999 argument that museums were experiencing a paradigmatic shift from "being *about* something to being *for* someone" (Weil, 1999). Weil's argument was in response to perceived transformational changes in museums as cultural institutions. One of these significant changes was in museums moving from object-centered institutions focused on providing cultural heritage information to an uninformed visitor to institutions focused on visitors with a goal of empowering them to function as change agents.

To be a people-centered institution would require museums to care about people. Caring for people demands caring about issues central to their lives. As such, the racial climate within the United States in the past several years (with the murders of Eric Garner, Trayvon Martin, George Floyd, Breonna Taylor, et al.) has caused museums to ask to what degree they can or should be relationally accessible amid national conversations and initiatives regarding racial inclusion, diversity, and social justice. As museums continue to join in solidarity movements by declaring Black Lives Matter, there is a growing movement that calls for museums to meet the demands for relational accessibility by creating a model of inclusion to reflect an emerging philosophy of museum as public forum. While the public seems to expect and demand that the museum space transform to accommodate public discourse on difficult conversations, some museums are still questioning if this can or should be the role of museums in the twenty-first century. If Black lives truly do matter, museums must demonstrate this by having Black lives serve on museum boards; they must promote, recruit, and retain Black leadership; and they must commit to stop policing Black bodies in White-facing institutions even as they must divest from the police. These efforts must be understood and executed as being racially literate acts that are not performative. The typology of action spawned from national conversations regarding race highlights how cultural responsiveness inevitably misses the mark if there is not a concrete understanding of the role that race and structural racism plays in museums.

Whiteness

An additional limit of inclusion as it relates to interrogating race is understanding the specificity and pervasiveness of Whiteness. Cynthia Levine-Rasky, author of *Whiteness Fractured*, writes that, "as members of society, we all participate in social institutions that identify and respond to different groups of people. We do so by drawing upon historical and current meanings of such groups" (2016, p. 3). When identity groups collectively affirm and replicate these meanings they are effectively reproduced within institutions, by the systems within social networks, and by people who move about in them, implementing popular meanings in their interactions. Levine-Rasky argues that while we are likely to think of non-White groups as part of a social construction, Whiteness is just as likely to not be regarded as such. Historically, people of color have been associated within societal networks as undesired, troubled, or problematic groups with a set of cultural norms, behaviors, and practices that equate to enormous difference. As such, the idea of Whiteness was further created and reinforced to counter the differences of non-White groups in such a way as to pronounce these differences as utterly opposite, if not, abnormal. In this manner, societal and cultural capital became racialized and used as a mechanism to exact power, with Whiteness existing as a means to measure the value of this difference.

Shannon Sullivan shapes an understanding of the ways that White privilege, the measurable power of racialized difference between groups identified as Whites and non-Whites, might be understood within cultural heritage institutions. Shannon writes in *Revealing Whiteness: The Unconscious Habits of Racial Privilege* (2006) that White privilege operates as unseen, invisible, even seemingly nonexistent and suggests that because of this hidden mode of operation, something more indirect than, and much different from conscious argumentation against White privilege is needed to combat it. The underlying assumptions of museum praxis are that these institutions advance, preserve, collect, and display the cultural heritage of all groups. However, Shannon's explication of the ways in which White privilege operates as "unseen," "invisible," and "seemingly nonexistent" do well to explain sentiments from many museum professionals still grappling with the fact that they do not possess the language or literacy to properly execute and apply practices that disrupt institutional racism in museums. In short, White privilege promotes the idea that the museum is a democratic space because it erases the architecture of structural racism. Shannon argues that White privilege operates as an unconscious habit. The unconscious habit is then only disrupted when visitors demand equity in presentation of cultural heritage or when museum professionals call out systemic and institutional racism within the structure. Museums respond by creating diversity initiatives, attempting to increase the types and number of programs and exhibitions that might appease or satisfy claims of exclusion. While many museums have genuine concern about repairing negative perceptions about museums as places *for* Whites and *about* Whites and not *about* or *for* people of color, inclusion policies are merely new ways to repeat old cycles of hopes for increasing diversity. If museums are to approach transformative change the way that Stephen Weil outlines, then inclusion must not be used as a blanket term and unpacking racism must come first.

Conclusion

If museums and museum professionals are not centering antiracist work, then inclusion is not possible. Furthermore, it is imperative that the term "inclusion" not be so swiftly interchangeable as to lose its meaning and focus. Inclusion is a strategy. It is not a blanket term to be coded out and switched to insert the "demographic" of the day. Queer Jamaican poet Staceyann Chin reminds us that "all oppression is connected."[3] And if we recognize that oppression exists, then labor toward inclusion must always be intersectional and residing squarely in the middle of transformation. So if you want to address the needs of people with physical disabilities or queer families or refugee communities you cannot do so without also understanding that caring about disabled visitors must also mean that you care about Black lives, must also mean that you care about Indigenous women's lives, must also mean that you care about teenagers, senior citizens, single mothers, _____ (insert identity).

FIGURE 2.1
A visual reminder of the interconnected nature of oppressive ideas and actions originally painted on the walls of the first home of the Nest Collective, a multidisciplinary arts collective, in Nairobi, Kenya. The original mural was inspired by the poetry of Jamaican artist and activist Staceyann Chin. This image now exists only in digital form and can be accessed online at https://www.jimchuchu.com/oppression.
Credit: Jim Chuchu https://www.jimchuchu.com/oppression

We want to be very clear about these statements. First, the work of inclusion begins at the institutional level regarding education, care, and commitment to disrupting institutional racism and thereby eradicating its practices for and by museum professionals. Antiracism is the commitment to the work of examining how museums function behind the scenes and what must be done to eradicate replications of systemic racism inside the institution. Next, in centering antiracism museums must repair the ways in which collections, interpretive material, marketing, and programming have or continue to exclude and other.

Inclusion can't exist without antiracism.

The limits of inclusion are maximized when museums and their professionals ignore the role that race and racism plays in literally all aspects of life.

Key Questions

1. What is your personal race narrative?
2. Where are you in the margins? What intersections and identities are most critical for you to unpack as you commit to this work?
3. Where are the limits of imagination for you in this work? What are your personal responsibilities to reshape and reframe these limits?
4. Who are you accountable to in this work?
5. What are three critical actions that you can take now to shift institutional and communal reality?
6. Name at least one institutional practice in museums that is inherently racist, ageist, ableist, homophobic, classist, etc. Name it as a form of oppression.

Notes

1. From an interview conducted at Boggs's home in Detroit, Michigan, July 22, which later appeared in print in "'Revolution as a New Beginning': An Interview with Grace Lee Boggs" Upping the Anti No. 1. p. 28. March 31, 2005. http://web.archive.org/web/20070415072944/http://oat.tao.ca/~tom/journal/uta1_sequential.pdf.

2. This speech made by Michelle Obama at the Whitney was the subject, and start-ing point, for a series of three blogposts featured on The Incluseum in 2015. https:// incluseum.com/2015/05/12/michelle-obama-activism-and-museum-employment-part-i/.

3. Staceyann Chin's spoken word poem "All Oppression is Connected" performed live. https://www.youtube.com/watch?v=4XfvZPG32-g.

Bibliography

Ahmed, Sara. "'You end up doing the document rather than doing the doing': Diver-sity, Race Equality and the Politics of Documentation." *Ethnic and Racial Studies* 30, no. 4 (2007): 590–609.

———. *On Being Included: Racism and Diversity in Institutional Life.* Durham, NC: Duke University Press, 2012.

brown, adrienne maree. *Emergent Strategy: Shaping Change, Changing Worlds.* Chico, CA: AK Press, 2017.

Chasmar, Jessica. "Michelle Obama Says Black Kids Feel Unwelcome at Museums; Cul-tural Institutions." *Washington Times*, May 6, 2015. https://www.washingtontimes .com/news/2015/may/6/michelle-obama-says-black-kids-feel-unwelcome-in-m/.

Harris, William, and Auntaneshia Staveloz. "AAM's Diversity and Inclusion Policy Statement Part I and II." *The Incluseum*, August 25, 2014. http://incluseum.com/ 2014/08/25/aams diversityandinclusion-policy-statement/.

Kelley, Robin D. G. *Freedom Dreams: The Black Radical Imagination.* Boston: Beacon Press, 2002.

Levine-Rasky, Cynthia. *Whiteness Fractured.* New York: Routledge, 2016.

Sullivan, Shannon. *Revealing Whiteness: The Unconscious Habits of Racial Privilege.* Bloomington: Indiana University Press, 2006.

Weil, Stephen. "From Being about Something to Being for Somebody: The Ongoing Transformation of the American Museum." *Daedalus* 128, no. 3 (1999): 229–58.

3

Opening Up to Transformation

A S WE HAVE ESTABLISHED IN CHAPTER 2, inclusion—as a concept, a word, and set of practices we enact in museums—is not an immutable value. It can be used by those seeking a rhetorical device to justify maintaining the status quo, such as the policies and practices that fortify racism, or, more broadly, to set limits around an organization's potential for change. But inclusion is also an *expansive* value. Through *The Incluseum*'s commitment to nuance inclusion and to collaboratively inquire about its potential for transforming the field, inclusion has served as a fruitful terrain for imagining new ideas and ways of working. Given the unique character of inclusion, and *The Incluseum*'s unique approach in going about understanding inclusion, we are now in a position to be able to share what we have learned to date about an approach to inclusion that can open the museum field up to transformation. We see these learnings as insights that have practical applications for museums seeking to meet their respective, fullest potential as relevant, engaged, and socially just entities deserving of community support and trust, now and for future generations.

An Emergent Paradigm

The Incluseum's content archive has been formed through almost ten years of grassroots, collaborative inquiry into what inclusion is and can be. The archive counts over two hundred entries contributed by nearly one hundred unique authors, also referred to as contributors. However, the fruits of this collaborative inquiry might not be readily legible to users or contributors to the platform. The blog format highlights the newest content, while the archive continues to expand in depth and scope with each contributor. Only those closest to the *Incluseum* platform, such as cofounders, frequent contributors, advisors, or longtime readers, likely retain a cumulative sense of what *Incluseum* content, and by extension the platform itself, has come to represent as an approach and orientation toward understanding inclusion in museums. In order to bring the *Incluseum*'s approach to inclusion into sharper relief, and to better communicate what this platform can teach us about inclusion in museums, we realized we must analyze *The Incluseum*'s content across time. To guide this process, we asked ourselves the following question: What insights into the state of practice pertaining to inclusion in US museums does *The Incluseum*'s content provide?

In dialogue with Porchia and Aletheia, Rose undertook an analysis of *The Incluseum*'s archive as part of her doctoral research (Paquet, 2021).[1] Her analysis identified four themes that were repeated across time in the archive:

- Relationships
- Social Justice
- Representation and Access
- Institutional Change

All four themes are deeply interconnected and best understood as being part of one another, as constituting a whole, like directional points. Together, these themes—and subthemes within—offer us a new paradigm by which we can orient ourselves toward inclusion in museums. Through its potential to counter the limits of imagination, discussed in the previous chapter, we propose that this paradigmatic framework brilliantly illuminates, and guides us closer to, the subject of our platform's collective dreaming, *The Incluseum*. As such, it is a paradigm salient in navigating us beyond the concept of "inclusion" itself and toward alternative realities—the opening up of today's museum field to transformation. In the following sections, we will expand on each of the four themes, providing concrete examples from the archive and drawing connections among these themes to illustrate how they interact with each other and invite transformation.

Table 3.1

Thematic Schema of *Incluseum* Blogpost Analysis

Relationships	Social Justice	Representation and Access	Institutional Change
Establishing partnerships and building relationships — External partnerships — Internal partnerships — Prioritizing collaboration and cocreation — Responding to contemporary events	**Dynamics of Power and Oppression** **Institutional Legacies** **The Self**	**Narrative Production** — Ceding representational control — Presenting new and counter-narratives — Interventions in permanent or temporary gallery spaces — Collections	**Necessitates a Strategy** **Take Stock: Institutional Assessment** **Make Investments**
Values — Trust building — Reciprocity — Authenticity — Accountability — Welcome — Listening — Shared authority — Transparency — Long-term commitment — Empathy — Equity	**Theoretical Lenses** — Critical race theory — Human rights	**Access** **Outreach** — Pop-up museums and museum without walls — Exhibitions and programs at partner organizations — Collection-based	
Emphasis on Process **Theoretical Lens** — Intercultural dialogue		**Employment**	

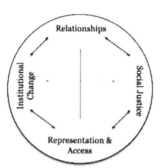

FIGURE 3.1
Relational Matrix of Inclusion

Theme One: Relationships

Of the four overarching themes identified through our analysis of *The Incluseum* archive, the theme of **Relationships** is unique. A value-centric, care-centered, and process-oriented ethos is fundamental to understanding this theme. The potential of this theme, among others that emerged in our analysis, is that ethics and values can ground us across our unique situations and contexts with an internal wisdom center. Across the other themes that emerged in our analysis—Social Justice, Representation and Access, and Institutional Change—we find echoes of this relationship-driven core. In this section we will delve into different dimensions of Relationships discussed in the archive, including eleven key values that guide this relational core.

The How of Relationships

Establishing partnerships and building relationships is discussed within the archive as occurring with various stakeholders outside and inside of the museum, either onsite or offsite. These partnerships and relationships spanned those with other organizations, community members, artists, colleagues within the field, and colleagues within a museum. The rationale for establishing partnerships and building relationships has been, at times, implied and explicitly stated other times. Aspects of this rationale include:

1. recognition of a knowledge-based deficit when it comes to working with new stakeholders (for example, how do stakeholders want to engage if at all, and how do they perceive the museum?),
2. recognition that new stakeholders are the best situated to inform what engagement is best suited for them, and

3. recognition that bridging expertise across stakeholder groups builds new possibilities and capacity for impact.

The archive provides examples of partnerships that are short and long term, on- and offsite, and that take place through many museum departments including collections, exhibitions, and education.

One example of offsite partnership comes from the Northwest African American Museum (NAAM) described in the blogpost "Pullman Porter Blues: Voices Amplified" (Wittman and Carter, 2012). Here, the museum decided to work with the Seattle Repertory Theatre to create an exhibition in conjunction with the play *Pullman Porter Blues* by playwright Cheryl L. West. The exhibition brought together museum artifacts related to Pullman Porters and Maids and was hosted in the theater lobby, thus creating a bridge between the two organizations and amplifying the topic from a multimodal perspective. Reflecting on this partnership, Brian Carter, former deputy director of education at NAAM, stated,

> I was proud to collaborate with the Seattle Rep on this project to explore the often overlooked stories of our community's Pullman Porters and Maids. Aligned partnerships are a necessity for museums in a climate of shrinking resources, fierce competition for audience attention and a changing world that demands we tell a more inclusive version of our shared human story.

Here, Carter uses the words "aligned partnerships" to describe these types of mutually beneficial engagements that leverage, connect, and amplify partners' unique assets.

Internal partnerships, which tend to be the lesser emphasized partnership type in museum literature and communications, are those that take place among colleagues within a museum with the goal of building capacity for inclusion. For example, in the blogpost "Engaging Latino Audiences at the Denver Art Museum: My First Year as the Latino Cultural Programs Coordinator" (Salazar, 2013), Madalena Salazar, former Latino cultural programs coordinator at the Denver Art Museum, described her role as follows:

> I plant kernels of ideas around the institution to get everyone thinking of how they can serve the needs of Latino audiences through their own role in the museum. The reality is that there isn't a simple solution for museums to implement in view of making a particular audience segment become more engaged on-site. I could not, in my role as an educator, do all that it takes to meet the needs of these audiences. I can, however, listen to our audiences' needs, implement what I can, and encourage other members of the institution to do their part. This, in my opinion, is what makes a museum inclusive. Inclusion requires everyone's efforts.

Here, Salazar understands her role as "planting kernels" across the museum so that considering Latino audiences and their needs can become a part of everyone's job. In other words, she sees it as her responsibility to build capacity internally for greater inclusion, which she understands as requiring "everyone's efforts." Other blogposts amplify this idea that internal partnership is akin to capacity building, adding that being grounded in trust, along with shared goals and commitments, is crucial for the success of this work.

Integral to the overarching practice of establishing partnerships and building relationships is **prioritizing collaboration and cocreation**. While all partnerships are not necessarily collaborative, collaborative partnerships entail working with the partnering stakeholders in the process of creating outputs. Cocreation takes this a step further and connotes a deeper engagement, a commitment to envision and create with partnering stakeholders.

For Chieko Phillips and Leilani Lewis, collaboration was a key commitment of their work at NAAM. In their blogpost "Responding to the Events in Ferguson and Beyond: The Northwest African American Museum's Example" (2014), Phillips, former exhibition manager, and Lewis, former creative arts administrator at NAAM, attribute the success of their responsiveness to contemporary events to their reputation as a collaborative institution. They state,

> We place a high value on our ability to collaborate and have worked diligently, and sometimes cumbersomely, for six years to improve our practice and solidify our reputation as a collaborative institution. As a young museum opened in 2008, we are still shaping our identity and practice of actualizing our mission. Our identity and survival is dependent on reciprocal participation with our audiences and communities. Our passionate, professionally trained, multicultural, and multigenerational staff of twelve advances our mission with a mutual understanding of the vitality of relevancy and collaborative practices. We develop multidisciplinary programming with the explicit intent to create a safe space where all can come to understand new issues and concepts.

Here, we see that for the NAAM, collaboration is about "vitality and relevancy" and helps to create a safe space for stakeholders to "understand new issues and concepts."

As illustrated in the previous example from the NAAM, **responding to contemporary events**, both national and regional, also emerged as an important aspect of museums being partners and in relationship with local stakeholders. This subtheme was mostly discussed in relation to the many visible instances of police brutality that took place across the country over the past decade. Whether or not to respond, and how to respond, were questions that many museums grappled with. The idea of "taking a stance" held many back, as the myth of neutrality still has a strong hold across the field. The importance of the response being timely emerged as well as it requiring flexibility.

Key Values Guiding Relationships

Throughout the archive, **eleven values** transpired as key to inclusion-related work. The contributors discussed these values to describe their approach to museum work, guiding the way they developed projects and worked with various stakeholders, especially those of marginalized backgrounds. Together, these eleven values give depth to the greater theme of Relationships and describe an ethical position from which relationships are centered, enacted, and cultivated. Overall, these values point to a different way of conducting museum work, one that is slower, centers caring relationships, and is based in an awareness of how the past is present as the future unfolds (that is, non-linear temporalities).

Many of these values are interconnected and are best understood as forming a web of values that coalesce into a conception of **Relationships** that is foundational to establishing partnerships and building relationships. In the following section we expand on this web of values and highlight their interconnections.

1. **Trust Building**

   Trust is described across the archive as a core value necessary to develop authentic relationships and collaborations with stakeholders. Authors discuss this value as taking time to cultivate, in other words, building trust is a process that cannot be rushed. Trust is linked to many other values, mainly transparency, authenticity, accountability, long-term commitment, listening, reciprocity, and respect.

2. **Reciprocity**

   Overall, the value of reciprocity is described by contributors as mutually beneficial exchanges and collaborations between a museum and community-based groups and members. This value is strongly linked to trust building and collaboration. As such, reciprocity is characterized as a value that reorients practice away from the extractive and exploitative modes of cultural production that were employed in the past and toward mutually beneficial outcomes.

3. **Authenticity**

   Although used in different contexts, this value is linked in the archive to the idea of something ringing true (for example, a narrative) and whose true motives are congruent with its rhetoric and behavior. Authenticity is about an institution showing up to "space-making" and inclusion efforts from a place of wanting to do the work and understanding that these efforts are not disassociated from the current historical and sociopolitical context of community members' lived realities. Authenticity is also linked to the quality of institutional narratives ringing true with local, community-based experiences and knowledges.

4. **Accountability**

Being accountable for institutional privileges is key to building trusting relationships with area residents and is linked to addressing systemic issues brought forth by marginalized peoples' experiences of museums. Accountability exists on an individual and interpersonal level, is called for at different levels of the institution, and exists in relation to the practices of allyship/accompliceship. The value of accountability is a practice, albeit not specifically detailed, that is called for within relationships. Individuals can be accountable for their thoughts and actions and as they engage in processes that aim to advance equity. Institutions can be accountable for past behavior and when building relationships that center trust. Individuals and institutions are accountable to those they are relating with.

5. **Welcome**

Welcome is a relational value linked to the broader concept of hospitality and is also a characteristic of a space. In the archive, welcome was mostly written about in terms of museums welcoming people of different backgrounds, and the ensuing changes in perception and practice this necessitates. Welcoming entails designing spaces and experiences that unsettle what any particular group of people expects the space to be like, thereby creating something that can better suit a plurality of experiences. Centering the very people museums wish to welcome in defining what welcome looks and feels like is crucial for creating such spaces.

6. **Listening**

Listening entails receptivity to hearing what life is like for other people than ourselves along with those we most closely relate to due to subjective positionality and life experiences. As with other values, listening is especially linked to museums working with oppressed and marginalized stakeholders. Listening is related to practices that rely on soliciting feedback such as evaluations and iterative approaches to program development. Listening is a key value to being in relation. Listening involves centering somebody else's truth and being receptive to hearing it.

7. **Shared Authority**

   Sharing authority entails decentering the museum as the sole holder and creator of knowledge and highlights the importance of cocreating outputs with noninstitutional stakeholders. From this value derives an ethical position that outputs ought to be created with stakeholders rather than for or about them. The value of shared authority is strongly connected to cocreation and collaboration. In fact, cocreation hinges on shared authority. It rests on the willingness to see noninstitutionally affiliated stakeholders as experts. As such, the role of the museum professional becomes that of a facilitator of multiple knowledges rather than sole content expert or producer. This might entail being open to what the final output can be and look like, releasing control over how the final product is shared or not within the exhibition, or educators taking a receptive and open stance regarding the experiences they are facilitating.

8. **Transparency**

   Transparency is linked closely across the archive to building trust. Likewise, it is linked to the necessary acknowledgment of how past institutional practices created harm and to implementing practices that aim to open up museum processes to both public participation and scrutiny.

9. **Long-Term Commitment**

   We see across the archive that the investment of time that is necessary to build trusting relationships is not a process that can be rushed. This connects to the value of authenticity, in that long-term investments mitigate the potential of perpetuating tokenizing modes of relating.

10. **Empathy**

    The nuances of empathy emerge in how it is discussed across the archive, applying to both individual and institutional contexts. It can be an organizing value, a practice of connecting people, a means to critique apathy and resist oppressive systems. Cautions and limitations to the value are also raised in the archive, suggesting that empathy might require an explicit framing in order to resist interpretations of the value that promote a savior mentality and enable achieving true social change.

11. **Equity**
    This value is represented in the archive as attuned to historical forces
    that have contributed to the contemporary status quo that has privi-
    leged some groups over others. Related to the situatedness of the value
    of equity within a broader context of systemic oppression, the archive
    emphasizes that equity is often associated with (social) justice. Enacted
    equity, if not situated within an overarching commitment to disman-
    tling oppressive systems, may remain superficial. Therefore a commit-
    ment to equity hinges on museum professionals engaging in critical
    self-awareness, iteratively envisioning, and rebuilding.

What makes these relational values so important, both in understanding
relationships as well as orienting ourselves to inclusion? Many contributors
situate their work within a greater understanding of how power dynamics
and legacies of oppression and exclusion shape contemporary museological
concerns for serving a wider audience and working with various communities
(especially nondominant ones). Relational values thus constitute an ethical
foundation from which to enact museum work otherwise, emphasizing care
and sensitivity to power dynamics and legacies of oppression, exploitation,
and exclusion. In other words, this web of values guides action and extends
to the following three themes. As stated earlier, foregrounding these values
decenters the primacy and urgency surrounding the development of museum
outputs (for example, exhibition, program), centering instead *the quality of
relationships cultivated in the process of product development*. For this reason,
we propose that **Relationships** is the theme that gives *The Incluseum*'s emergent paradigm its "true North," an ethical grounding through which, if we
ever get off track, we can reset and recalibrate to move forward.

Theme Two: Social Justice

The theme of Social Justice presented itself in different ways across *Incluseum*
contributor entries—explicit mentions of "social justice" and more nuanced
aspects of social justice emerged. Overall, we found that the theme of Social
Justice expressed itself in three overlapping ways throughout *The Incluseum*
archive—Dynamics of Power and Oppression, Institutional Legacies, and
Self. These are in line with Alyssa Machida's description of the three overlapping "terrains" of power that museum professionals navigate in their daily
work, namely, the global, institutional, and the self (2016). Machida, former
interpretive specialist at the Detroit Institute of Art, explains that each of
these terrains present unique ecologies that must be unpacked and understood separately and in relation to each other. Following her work, we link
the archive's three subthemes pertaining to social justice to these terrains.[2]

Dynamics of Power and Oppression

Within *The Incluseum* archive, the subtheme **Dynamics of Power and Oppression [Global Terrain]** entails developing an understanding for how the concept of oppression can be reinforced unconsciously (microaggressions, bias, etc.) and be rooted in past injustices (slavery, genocide, colonialism and institutional policies/practices/codes that are structured to exclude some groups). Social justice also entails a focus on ensuring everyone equitable access to resources in society, including museums, as well as how injustices are reinforced and reified in institutional policies.

For example, in his blogpost "Oppression: A Museum Primer" (2015), nikhil trivedi, director of engineering for a museum in Chicago and social justice activist, defines oppression as follows:

> Oppression is "the act of one social group using power or privilege for its own benefit while disempowering, marginalizing, silencing and subordinating another group."[3]

He continues,

> When we benefit from power we have privilege, when we are dominated by power we are targets of oppression. Within this context of power, privilege is **an advantage or benefit enjoyed by one group at the expense of others**. Oppression is **the domination of one group of people for the benefit of another group of people**. Domination can take many forms, including limiting or removing the power of a person or group (disempowering), treating a person or group as insignificant (marginalizing), prohibiting or preventing voices from being heard (silencing) and regarding a person or group as less important or dependent (subordinating).

Connected to museums in particular, he states,

> Thinking about our field, who has the capacity to control circumstances when museums acquire or display objects from ancient civilizations, particularly when their descendants are still active in our communities?
> The work to end oppression, particularly within institutions whose histories are inextricably linked with slavery, genocide and colonialism, can feel overwhelming. . . . We can all learn, grow, and participate in the movements to end oppression. It won't end for anyone until it ends for everyone, and there's plenty of space for us to have an impact.

trivedi offers other examples of institutional oppression in his blogpost "Oppression: A Museum Primer—Update" (2016). He states,

In our institutions, lots of people are involved in everything we do. Institutional oppression is when our museums engage with marginalized people in dominating ways, and no one in our institutions have the power to speak up, or to be heard. For example, is there a gallery in your museums that documents American or European history that doesn't feature any people of color? If they are featured, are they addressed by their names? People of color and our identities have systematically been erased from our histories, dominating them with white narratives. Has this gallery been acknowledged and talked about in your institution? Those feelings of an elephant in the room that no one feels comfortable bringing up are good indicators of where institutional oppression may be operating in your museum.

We noted that Dynamics of Power and Oppression take place along intersecting axes that have long-standing histories and structure our society. Four of these axes are discussed by contributors, namely, Race, Gender and Sexuality, Ability, and Immigration. Moreover, several blogposts mention or treat with more depth the realities of White supremacy culture and colonialism under which each of these intersecting axes coalesce. White supremacy culture is represented as a norm that is marked by a state of "unconsciousness" to those who benefit from this culture. White supremacy is also discussed as more complex than a Black-White binary and must account for the diversity of ways in which oppression occurs across many complex identities.

Further entries from contributors to *The Incluseum* archive mention White privilege and refer to museums as "public white spaces" that represent the "dominant culture" through erasures of other cultures. Importantly, these manifestations of White privilege are linked to negative outcomes such as trauma. As a result, museums are called on to dismantle and decenter Whiteness, paying close attention to how Whiteness is embedded in work practices. As we will see in the next subtheme, White supremacy culture is a subject well-represented in *The Incluseum* archive for its long history of shaping our society and its institutions, as well as our individual and collective identities.

Institutional Legacies

The next subtheme, **Institutional Legacies [Institutional Terrain]**, comprises the conditions under which the Western museum originated and continues, in large part, to operate. The emphasis on how these past legacies have shaped and continue to determine the present scope of possibilities is exemplified and emphasized in Alyssa Machida's writing. In "The Dreamspace Project: A Critical Workbook and Toolkit for Critical Praxis in the American Art Museum Part 2" (2016b), she states,

> The American art museum and its historic and contemporary practices of collecting, categorizing, defining, and marginalizing cultures and peoples from around the world under the guise of aesthetic excellence is highly political, operating from legacies of colonialism and a global system of White Supremacy. Legacies are not only historically fabricated, but persistently and currently upheld by our own (in)actions and (in)decisions. The term "White Supremacy" might bring to mind certain imagery, groups, or moments from history, but it is used here to refer to the global system of power that privileges White property, capital, values, ideals, and peoples. The construction of dominance necessitates subordination: the oppressed, colonized, enslaved, marginalized, Other-ized, racialized, dehumanized, and disenfranchised. We must always keep this duality and reification of power in mind.

Here, Machida makes it explicit that "legacies are not only historically fabricated, but persistently and currently upheld by our own (in)actions and (in) decisions," thus emphasizing the enduring nature of legacies from past to present. Moreover, this continuity perpetuates the fact that "the construction of dominance necessitates subordination," in other words, perpetuation of the structures of power.

A crucial aspect of working within this precarious terrain of Institutional Legacies is linked to the value of Trust discussed earlier. Contributors indicate that building trust is a crucial first step for museums interested in greater inclusion because it entails honestly reckoning with institutional legacies of exclusion, exploitation, colonization, and theft that continue to limit who museums are for and perpetuate feelings of mistrust resulting from these harmful legacies. Institutional Legacies of colonialism are very much alive in museum collections and exhibitions, bearing significant impact on visitors, especially those whose ancestors were dominated, oppressed, and stolen from.

An example of this connection between Trust and Institutional Legacies comes from contributor Chris Taylor, former director of inclusion and community engagement at the Minnesota Historical Society in his blogpost "Announcing the Department of Inclusion and Community Engagement at the Minnesota Historical Society: Part II" (2015). In reflecting on the process of founding the department of inclusion and community engagement, Taylor states,

> As a museum and an institution older than our state, we have a long history. Our relationships with diverse communities are often hindered by mistrust or negative perceptions. As most museums do, we have episodes in our past where we understand that we have not acted in the best interests of these communities. Recognizing our past, but even more than recognizing, acknowledging our past begins the healing process for some individuals in these communities. Developing inclusive practices that *build trust* with these communities allows MNHS

opportunities to engage communities in *authentic* and *mutually beneficial* ways. Building accountability mechanisms allows staff to engage communities as equal contributors and helps build the trust we need to become truly inclusive. (Emphasis in original)

Here, we see Taylor acknowledging that over the course of its long history, the Minnesota Historical Society (MNHS) acted in ways that created mistrust from different local communities, and that this mistrust was carried forward.[4] Only through recognizing *and* acknowledging the causes of this mistrust can the MNHS begin the process of healing relationships and building a more inclusive institution.

The Self

Finally, **The Self [Terrain of the Self]** emerged as another terrain of reflection and action within the social justice landscape. As discussed in chapter 2, the Self refers to the fact that museums, along with being social institutions that have inherited and continue to perpetuate certain legacies, are made up of individuals who are powerful actors in maintaining the status quo or creating change. As such, each museum professional is encouraged to self-reflect in order to grow critical self-awareness and take personal responsibility. As contributor Alyssa Machida writes in "The Dreamspace Project: A Critical Workbook and Toolkit for Critical Praxis in the American Art Museum Part I" (2016a),

With the Dreamspace Project, I take the approach that we can only truly extend ourselves as far as we have dared to examine and interrogate inward; to cast an eye not only upon the world and others, but to spend time critically studying ourselves and the many layers and identities we hold. I have come to realize that the bulk of the "work" we must engage in is primarily self-work.

Throughout the archive, the practices of increasing cultural competency and bias literacy were discussed as means to grow critical self-awareness. Entries also presented the idea of adopting an activist stance vis-à-vis social justice matters. This stance is a personal decision that can be leveraged to create action through, for example, the practices of ally/accompliceship and becoming an advocate for social justice causes.

Theme Three: Representation and Access to Museum Resources

The next main theme discussed in *The Incluseum* archive is **Representation and Access to Museum Resources**. This theme is focused on museums increasing who is represented and has access therein. In the archive, being represented is talked about in terms of seeing oneself—one's identity—in the museum (for example, in the collections, exhibitions, staff), and in terms of being represented in decision-making processes and narrative production. As such, representation is both an output and a process. This theme is important because it touches on who sees themselves as belonging to museum spaces or not. As contributor Emily Dawson, former lecturer at University College, London, states in "Why Think about Equity in Museums" (2015),

> If museums and similar institutions are valuable resources for our societies, telling important stories through objects, programmes, exhibits and so on, then those stories reflect how we see ourselves, how we construct knowledge, power and relevance. Designing stories where some people are "in" while others are firmly "out," "other" or "invisible" is a form of oppression. So representation matters in terms of building a sense of who matters, whose knowledge matters, whose stories matter (and so on) in our societies.

The theme of **Representation and Access to Museum Resources** is concerned with the *how* and *what* of representation and access. In other words, this theme is equally concerned with the *processes* of representation and access, as well as its *outputs*. As such, outputs that do not reflect processes attuned to **Relationships** and **Social Justice** will not be aligned with inclusion. It should be noted that representation and access are two entwined concepts; increased representation is a form of access and vice versa.

Four subthemes related to **Representation and Access to Museum Resources** were discussed in the archive. These are Narrative Production, Access, Outreach, and Employment, which we go on to discuss next.

Narrative Production

As the title of this subtheme indicates, **Narrative Production** is concerned with both the narratives presented in museums and their production. As such, it is focused on *processes* and *outputs*. In the archive, *processes* were discussed in terms of *ceding representational control* to either a multivocal group charged with narrative production or to those being centered in the representational output (that is, whose stories are being told). *Outputs* were discussed in terms of *presenting new and counter-narratives* within museum spaces that partially hinge on the material held in the museum's *collections*, because artifacts are used as one of the main sources of evidence that support the narratives being presented.

a. Ceding representational control

Ceding representational control takes as central the power embedded in creating/authoring narratives and calls on museums to move from the traditional practice of single authorship by an academic expert to practices that are multivocal, community-centered, and allow for self-representation. In the archive, self-representation is referred to as giving stakeholders "room to speak for themselves" (Wittman, 2012) and "telling stories in their own voice" (Hansen, 2017).

For example, Jaden Hansen, founder of the Museum of Minneapolis, explains in "On Creating the Museum of Minneapolis" (2017),

> I founded Museum of Minneapolis in 2014 in reaction to the lack of representation for marginalized communities in historical society collections and exhibitions. My previous position as an Executive Director for a prominent county historical society, showed me the tremendous impact that creating space for people to tell their stories in their own voices has on community.

For Hansen, the importance of allowing stakeholders to self-represent was the impetus for founding the Museum of Minneapolis. Moreover, this impetus was reinforced by the lack of representation in museum collections and archives.

Moreover, contributors discussed how ceding representational control begins with the pertinent question "whose story told by whom" (Callihan, 2018) and proceeds to a critical stance of the institutional perspectives "these stories are filtered through" (Taylor, 2015). As Chris Taylor states in "Announcing the Department of Inclusion and Community Engagement at the Minnesota Historical Society: Part II,"

> It is time to democratize the stories we tell and the perspectives we filter them through. We must recognize and celebrate the contributions and narratives of all Minnesotans and indigenous people from this region at our museums and historic sites. It is incumbent upon us to work with our constituents to seek out new information and transform existing narratives to better reflect the demographics of the state. We must also create a welcoming atmosphere for all visitors at our sites and museums by utilizing culturally relevant interpretation and presentation techniques. (2015)

Culturally relevant interpretation and presentation techniques can be supported through community-centered, self-representational practices such as community advisory committees where stakeholders contribute their expertise from "concept to closing" (Greenberg, 2015).

Importantly, and as discussed in several blogposts, the role of the curator or exhibition designer shifts when a museum chooses to employ self-representational and community-based practices. Aligning with the relational and process-oriented nature of these practices, the role of the curator or exhibition designer was characterized as becoming a facilitator of multiple voices, perspectives, and experiential knowledges rather than being a single author. Outputs of this process are thus twofold: (1) strong(er) relationships among exhibition contributors, as well as between the museum and contributors, and (2) the exhibition itself.

b. Presenting new and counter-narratives

Moreover, throughout the archive, the exhibition-as-output was discussed in terms of presenting new and counter-narratives that lead to interventions in permanent or temporary gallery spaces. Here, exhibitions were described as powerful modalities for challenging the status quo and dominant narratives, or "bringing to public view" work that "makes the community confront difficult truths about itself" (Garfinkle, 2012).

Challenging the status quo can also be done through presenting new and counter-narratives that value and validate the cultures of marginalized groups. This can serve an important purpose for those who hold the identities being presented and can be described as a means of "claiming space" and "infiltrating archives and collections" because of a gap in the institutional record (Bailey, 2012). For example, in reflecting on her project Queering the Museum (QTM) in The Road to Revealing Queer: An Interview with Curator Erin Bailey, Part I" (Greenslit and Bailey, 2014), Erin Bailey, cofounder of QTM, states,

> This exhibition is a lot like a reunion of memories, which is very important for validating and authenticating people's lived experiences . . . and the fact that this is all happening in a museum makes it a part of the greater narrative.

Overall, the power in presenting new and counter-narratives underscores whose memory and stories are considered valid, which in turn impacts how we view each other in the present and shapes our collective memory of ourselves, places, and events.

c. Collections

Collections also emerged as a significant factor under Narrative Production. Narrative Production is discussed as either being hindered or aided by the presence of artifactual evidence in museum collections and archives. Going back to Jaden Hansen's blog "On Creating the Museum of Minneapolis," he states,

What becomes increasingly clearer as our communities acknowledge the problem with the homogenization of history, is that not everyone is able to find relevance in current exhibitions or even the museum archives. Important stories about Chinese immigrants, African-Americans, and Latino neighborhoods, for example, go unfinished because the archives don't exist to support an exhibition. Or rather, the records had never been added to the archives in the first place. Historical societies tend to be long established organizations, which gives them the power to shape the narratives of the communities they reside in due to the collections they hold in the public's trust. The historical societies come to facilitate representation.

As Hansen explains, the lack of representation of marginalized groups within museums' and historical societies' archives limits inclusion of the stories these sites are able to tell and present.

The Incluseum entries also suggest that there are many ways in which this limitation can be addressed, such as collection development strategies aimed at attuning museums' collections to the local demographics, whether historical or recently shifting. In other cases, artifactual evidence may already exist to assist in narrative production, but it is either incorrectly recorded or lacks a direct connection to source communities. Both instances hinder the artifacts' potential to be utilized in effective narrative production.

For example, in "(Re)Connection in Collaboration: Zuni Collection Reviews at the Indian Arts Research Center (IARC)," Patricia Baudino (2014), former intern at the IARC, discusses how the IARC developed collection-based collaborations to reconnect source communities with cultural materials and reestablish source community control over objects and knowledge. As a result, she writes that "this era of respect and collaboration has reorganized traditional hierarchies of knowledge and power, inspired indigenous-centered collection care, and created sites for community sharing and cultural support." Moreover, these collaborations have also resulted in correcting "inaccurate information within the IARC records" and "added Zuni names for objects, creating more dynamic, layered, and Zuni-appropriate records." Shifting dynamics of knowledge and power can have a significant impact on the possibilities of narrative production, ensuring source community investment/power and more accurate representation of people and cultural material.

Access

Across *Incluseum* entries, **access** was discussed particularly in terms of various barriers that prevent access and need to be attended to. Four specific types of access are presented across the archive. These include:

- Physical Access
- Cognitive/Intellectual Access
- Financial Access
- Linguistic Access

Outreach

In *The Incluseum* archive, **Outreach** was discussed as museum activities that took place outside of the museum's "four walls." These activities tend to engage stakeholders in creative ways that are not constrained by the need to physically travel to and be in a museum. Moreover, they leveraged the potential held by hosting exhibitions and programs at partner organizations in terms of connecting and engaging with new stakeholders. As such, these time-bound activities lead to experiments in the location in which a museum is sited and performed (for example, storefronts, shopping centers) and thus result in innovative ways to increase representation and access to museum resources. Whether or not and how these activities then impact the physical and enduring museum was not the focus of the discussion represented across entries but is a question we hold.

Across entries, all outreach activities discussed are free to the participant stakeholders. An example of this type of outreach activity is the pop-up museum. The pop-up museum is a time-bound event that is also thematically bound and contingent on participants contributing "their own personal objects and stories in order to create conversation and build community" (Delcarlo, 2012). Originally designed by Michelle Delcarlo, former Spark!Lab national network coordinator at the Smithsonian, the pop-up museum was later built upon by the Museum of Art and History (MAH) in Santa Cruz, California, as a method to collaborate with community partners and bridge different communities with the institutional context. As Nora Grant, former community programs coordinator at the MAH, writes in "Pop-Up Museums in Santa-Cruz" (2014),

> We work in collaboration with community partners to choose a theme and venue, and invite people to bring something on-topic to share. We lay out tables with empty frames and museum labels. When participants show up, they write a label for their object and leave it on display. You can also think of pop up

museums as potluck museums, because everyone is invited to bring something to share. The museum lasts for a few hours on one day and people can take their items home with them whenever they please.

Pop up museums typically take place outside of our museum, and at the site of our collaborating partner or organization. . . .

One of the reasons we started the pop up museum project was to challenge the idea that museums have an omnipresent authority over what is and what's not "valuable." We were surprised to learn though that the pop up museum is actually most compelling when we exhibit objects from the museum's collection alongside individuals' objects. This bridges institutional and community-created content. By sharing the same space, you're illustrating how a personal object can have just as much story value as a museum object.

In this example, we see connections to other themes discussed earlier, namely, establishing external partnerships, prioritizing collaboration and cocreation, building trust, and sharing authority.

The Incluseum archive also presented examples of *collection-based outreach*. This pertains to a pop-up museum event where museum artifacts were included as well as other examples where collections were the main vehicle for outreach. For instance, Sven Haakanson Jr., curator of Native American anthropology at the Burke Museum of Natural History, studies model *angyat* (kayaks of Sugpiat people of Kodiak, Alaska) stored in museums worldwide that he then reproduces and uses for hands-on teaching of *angyat* construction. His approach to working with museum collections exemplifies the potential of studying and sharing/repatriating knowledge embedded in cultural artifacts (Haakanson and Paquet, 2014). Additionally, collection-based outreach is expressed through prioritizing the development of a nimble, responsive method to connect collections to diverse civic stakeholders through, for example, traveling collection boxes (Erickson, 2015). The archive also speaks to the ways collection-based outreach can leverage digital modalities in innovative ways by identifying technologies already utilized by stakeholder groups that the museum wishes to engage with (for example, a radio show).

Employment

While the topic of employment will be discussed in greater depth in the following section on Institutional Change, it is included here as **employment**, along with internships and board opportunities, were discussed in the archive as important resources that museums hold and provide access to. *The Incluseum* entries discuss employment, internships, and board opportunities in general terms, for example, as needing to reflect the local community. For example, as Madalena Salazar shares in "Engaging Latino Audiences at the Denver Art Museum (DAM): My First Year as the Latino Programs Coordinator" (2013),

> The DAM has a history of being a comfortable and welcoming place, so I run into few road-blocks, thankfully. As usual, the major obstacles are resources and staffing. It only goes so far to act inclusively if an institution will not put its money where its mouth is, or diversify its staff makeup. I think that as cultural programs become more successful, and audience builds, there will be little choice but to make sure the staff reflects the make-up of the community, and funding proves that the institution supports all audiences equally.

For Salazar, that the staff makeup reflects the community is about the museum putting "its money where its mouth is" and "proves that the institution supports all audiences equally." However, several barriers to this access to employment exist. These are discussed in the next section on theme four.

Theme Four: Institutional Change

The final theme that emerged in our analysis of *The Incluseum* archive is **Institutional Change**. In truth, the first three themes are also about institutional change; shifting museum practice to center **Relationships** and **Social Justice** and attend to the complexities of increasing **Representation and Access** are fundamentally about institutional change. More than that, these three preceding themes are about a greater paradigmatic change—evolution, r-evolution, transformation—that encompasses all aspects of society. However, throughout the archive are many blogposts that deal with the theme of Institutional Change specifically and explicitly. In these entries, authors spoke of "in-reach," or of internal change, that is, change that produces transformation in the internal structures and cultures of museums so that they can be better positioned to accomplish the inclusion and equity ideals they aspire to externally. In "For the Love of Al Green: Revisiting Bunch's 'Flies in the Buttermilk' 15 Years Later" (2015), Porchia Moore (coauthor of this book) quotes Lonnie Bunch, the current fourteenth secretary of the Smithsonian Institution, saying,

> We champion the practice of community outreach. But I think we need to promote "in-reach," a concept that challenges the profession to be more introspective, more deliberate, more honest, and more explicit in its efforts to change itself.

Similarly, Alyssa Machida shares in "The Dreamspace Project: A Critical Workbook and Toolkit for Critical Praxis in the American Art Museum

Part 2" (2016b) that "what is necessary is the iterative process of criticality, envisioning, and rebuilding our practices and institutions upon fundamental values of inclusion and equity." And as Moore explains in "The Danger of the 'D' Word: Museums and Diversity" (2014), this work of internal change matters because

> We are the cultural gatekeepers. It matters who enters our gates. It matters what is inside our gates. It matters how our gates our perceived. We are tasked with making sure that our cultural heritage reaches all.

Museums have power and control over how they choose to wield this power. In the archive, the work of internal change was often discussed as encompassing an understanding of the themes and subtheme areas discussed earlier in this chapter, such as Dynamics of Power and Oppression, Institutional Legacies, and the Self. In other cases, internal change is discussed in terms of either shifting or creating new internal policies, procedures, and practices to support inclusion ideals.

Several *Incluseum* entries discussed the fact that inclusion, and its accompanying internal change, *necessitates a cross-departmental strategy*. These examples cover how the lack of an internal and external strategy creates internal tensions and a sense that efforts at inclusion were "pulling in different directions" (Taylor, 2015). What is needed instead is a holistic and cohesive set of strategies to be coordinated across departments that receive leadership support and are prioritized on all levels of the museum.

Throughout the archive, many different ideas and practices also cohered under the step to *Take Stock through Institutional Assessment*. These ideas included:

- consider current staff members' cultural competency and capacity for inclusion-related work;
- critically assess the museum's voice embedded in, for example, signage, marketing material, and exhibitions;
- become aware of unconscious biases and assumptions present on the individual and institutional level. These biases and assumptions are or become embedded in the museum voice;
- assess the internal culture;
- examine labor practices regarding internships, hiring, and staff retention, which connects to the previous point about internal culture:

  ○ What skills and qualifications are prioritized in job descriptions?
  ○ What is the pipeline to museum employment and is it equitable?;

- excavate institutional legacies (as elaborated on in the discussion of theme two earlier in the chapter); and
- probe institutional practices and policies.

Many of these points are, in fact, intimately connected. For instance, the "pipeline" to museum employment is tied to the internal culture, along with individual and institutional biases and assumptions about job qualifications.

Conclusion

Almost ten years of grassroots, collaborative inquiry into what inclusion is and can be through *The Incluseum*'s platform has resulted in a rich archive of collective knowledges of the various experiences and experimentations of colleagues in the field. Looking to *The Incluseum*'s archive as a whole, we wondered what key insights into the state of practice pertaining to inclusion in US museums would emerge. Through our analysis presented in this chapter, we found that four main themes emerged—Relationships, Social Justice, Representation and Access, and Institutional Change—each holding various insights of their own. Taken together, these four interconnected themes offer a tool for navigating our contemporary museum realities and encourage a move from power-over to power-with modes of relating based on the propositions that:

Inclusion is about care-centered relationships that center social justice to increase representation and access to museum resources and hinges on institutional change.

When the center or foundation of our work shifts, or it seems more possible for it to do so, we are in the process of transforming ourselves. This tool, this paradigm, is premised in a way of knowing about inclusion that entails attentiveness not only to the themes themselves, as lenses through which we understand inclusion, but also in our ability to tap into a new value-driven knowledge center that can beat at the heart of all we do in museums. In the next chapter, we contextually situate this paradigm in relation to the moment's current unfolding. We then explore how this paradigm can reorient our field's understanding and approach to inclusion and how to use it in forecasting and facilitating museum transformations within contemporary realities.

Key Questions

1. If asked, could you name your personal power? How does that power show up in the work that you do in and about museums?
2. What are care-centered practices that all museums and professionals who work in them should be engaged in and supporting?
3. What role does empathy play in how you work? Is there a place where professionalism and best practices create tensions or challenges for operating from within the framework of empathy?
4. What relationships and communities are most precious to you in the work of inclusion?
5. In what ways have you processed coping mechanisms and trauma that are possible residuals for working in museums?
6. What are the best aspects of museum work, and what specifics about the work that you do fill you with joy?

Notes

1. See Rose's published dissertation for more details on the methodology utilized to guide the analysis process. https://digital.lib.washington.edu/researchworks/bitstream/handle/1773/47599/Paquet_washington_0250E_22997.pdf?sequence=1.

2. For more on the intersection of museums with social justice objectives and potentials, see Gonzales, 2020.

3. See also http://www.ncra.ca/equity/ncra-anti-oppression-toolkit.pdf.

4. The Minnesota Historical Society was founded in 1849 by the territorial legislature almost a decade before statehood. See https://en.wikipedia.org/wiki/Minnesota_Historical_Society.

Bibliography

Bailey, Erin. "Queer Is Here and in Our Museums!" *The Incluseum*, September 20, 2012. https://incluseum.com/2012/09/20/queer-is-here-and-in-our-museums/.

Baudino, Patricia. "(Re)Connection in Collaboration: Zuni Collection Reviews at the Indian Arts Research Center (IARC)." *The Incluseum*, April 30, 2014. https://incluseum.com/2014/04/30/reconnection-in-collaboration-zuni-collection-reviews-at-the-indian-arts-research-center/.

Callihan, Elisabeth. "An Introduction to the Mass Action Toolkit from the Co-Founder." *The Incluseum*, July 13, 2018. https://incluseum.com/2018/07/23/an-introduction-to-the-mass-action-toolkit-from-the-co-founder/.

Dawson, Emily. "Why Think about Equity in Museums." March 23, 2015. https://incluseum.com/2015/03/23/why-think-about-equity-and-museums/.

Delcarlo, Michelle. "The Pop Up Museum as a Social Inclusion Strategy." *The Incluseum*, September 27, 2012. https://incluseum.com/2012/09/27/the-pop-up-museum-as-a-social-inclusion-strategy/.

Erickson, Rachel. "The Open Museum in Glasgow, Scotland." *The Incluseum*, November 16, 2015. https://incluseum.com/2015/11/16/open-museum-glasgow-scotland/.

Garfinkle, Robert. "Allyship and the Race Exhibit: Reflections Part 1." *The Incluseum*, December 6, 2012. https://incluseum.com/2012/12/06/allyship-and-the-race-exhibit-reflections-part-i/.

Gonzales, Elena. *Exhibitions for Social Justice.* London: Routledge, 2020.

Grant, Nora. "Pop-Up Museums in Santa-Cruz." *The Incluseum*, August 18, 2014. https://incluseum.com/2014/08/18/pop-up-museums-in-santa-cruz/.

Greenberg, Alyssa. "Two Takeaways from MuseumNext 2015." *The Incluseum*, October 7, 2015. https://incluseum.com/2015/10/07/two-takeaways-from-museumnext-2015/.

Greenslit, Jana, and Erin Bailey. "Queering the Museum in the Road to Revealing Queer: An Interview with Curator Erin Bailey, Part I." *The Incluseum*, March 5, 2014. https://incluseum.com/2014/03/05/the-road-to-revealing-queer-an-interview-with-curator-erin-bailey-part-i/.

Haakanson, Sven Jr., and Rose Paquet. "Repatriating Knowledge: Connecting Museums and Communities Part 1." *The Incluseum*, August 4, 2014. https://incluseum.com/2014/08/04/repatriating-knowledge-connecting-museums-and-communities/.

Hansen, Jaden. "On Creating the Museum of Minneapolis." *The Incluseum*, August 24, 2017. https://incluseum.com/2017/08/24/on-creating-the-museum-of-minneapolis/.

Machida, Alyssa. "The Dreamspace Project: A Workbook and Toolkit for Critical Praxis in the American Art Museum." 2016. https://incluseum.files.wordpress.com/2018/01/the-dreamspace-project-workbook.pdf.

———. "The Dreamspace Project: A Critical Workbook and Toolkit for Critical Praxis in the American Art Museum Part 1." *The Incluseum*, August 11, 2016a. https://incluseum.com/2016/08/11/a-workbook-and-toolkit-for-critical-praxis-in-the-american-art-museum/.

———. "The Dreamspace Project: A Critical Workbook and Toolkit for Critical Praxis in the American Art Museum Part 2." *The Incluseum*, October 13, 2016b. https://incluseum.com/2016/10/13/the-dreamspace-project-a-workbook-and-toolkit-for-critical-praxis-in-the-american-art-museum-part-2/.

Meikle, Emily. "Artifacts on Air." *The Incluseum*, December 13, 2016. https://incluseum.com/2016/12/13/artifacts-on-air/.

Moore, Porchia. "The Danger of the 'D' Word: Museums and Diversity." *The Incluseum*, January 20, 2014. https://incluseum.com/2014/01/20/the-danger-of-the-d-word-museums-and-diversity/.

———. "For the Love of Al Green: Revisiting Bunch's 'Flies in the Buttermilk' 15 Years Later." *The Incluseum*, April 24, 2015. https://incluseum.com/2015/04/23/for-the-love-of-al-green-revisiting-bunchs-flies-in-the-buttermilk-15-years-on/.

Paquet, Rose. *Cultivating Inclusion in U.S. Museums: Insights from the Incluseum.* ProQuestDissertations Publishing, 2021.

Phillips, Chieko, and Leilani Lewis. "Responding to the Events in Ferguson and Beyond: The Northwest African American Museum's Example." *The Incluseum*, December 16, 2014. https://incluseum.com/2014/12/16/responding-to-the-events-in-ferguson-and-beyond-the-northwest-african-american-museums-example/.

Salazar, Madalena. "Engaging Latino Audiences at the Denver Art Museum: My First Year as the Latino Cultural Programs Coordinator." *The Incluseum*, March 13, 2013. https://incluseum.com/2013/03/13/engaging-latino-audiences-at-the-denver-art-museum-my-first-year-as-the-latino-cultural-programs-coordinator/.

Taylor, Chris. "Announcing the Department of Inclusion and Community Engagement at the Minnesota Historical Society: Part II." *The Incluseum*, April 22, 2015. https://incluseum.com/2015/04/22/announcing-the-department-of-inclusion-and-community-engagement-at-the-minnesota-historical-society-part-ii/.

trivedi, nikhil. "Oppression: A Museum Primer." *The Incluseum*, February 4, 2015. https://incluseum.com/2015/02/04/oppression-a-museum-primer/.

———. "Oppression: A Museum Primer—Update." *The Incluseum*, September 16, 2016. https://incluseum.com/2016/09/19/oppression-a-museum-primer-update/.

Wittman, Aletheia. "Facing Homelessness: Skid Road at [Storefront] Olson Kunding Architects." *The Incluseum*, August 15, 2012. https://incluseum.com/2012/08/15/facing-homelessness-skid-road-storefront-olson-kundig/.

Wittman, Aletheia, and Brian Carter. "Pullman Porter Blues: Voices Amplified." *The Incluseum*, October 22, 2012. https://incluseum.com/2012/10/22/pullman-porter-blues-voices-amplified/.

4

Implications for the Field

A Period of Clarity

A T THE OUTSET OF THIS BOOK, in the preface, we situate ourselves as authors who have experienced the past two years (2020–2022) in many ways to which fellow museum and cultural workers might relate. Throughout the period of writing this book, we witnessed a field in crisis, museums across the nation closing their doors to in-person visitation without knowing when they might reopen—sometimes reopening, closing again, and reopening with no assurances of this cycle ending. It is within this context of uncertainty and upheaval that we considered the meaning and significance of the new, emergent paradigm for understanding inclusion we outlined in chapter 3. We asked ourselves what guidance this emergent paradigm can offer museum workers and leaders who must reckon with the past two years of tumult. As such, this chapter considers key ongoing developments within the field and society at large to situate, and demonstrate, the need for a paradigmatic shift in understanding inclusion and how *The Incluseum*'s emergent paradigm responds to that need.

As we move toward a de-escalated, but still uncertain reality, across the museum field—further from the start of the COVID-19 pandemic, further from the start of the racial justice uprising in the wake of George Floyd's brutal murder, further from the Trump administration and its violent final thralls—we have an opportunity to assess what has been revealed to us about the core values of our museum institutions. At times of urgency and emergency, when existential concerns arise, we often turn inward to our core values for guidance. We listen for their tones and cadences, as the din of doubts and demands tries to distract us. Really, all that museums have to guide them, in today's shifting museum landscape, are values. And if we didn't already know, where our museums choose to focus in these tense times can reveal to us a great deal about those spoken, or unspoken, values that operate at their core. Author Maya Angelou once remarked, "When someone shows you who they are, believe them the first time." We should believe our institutions as they tell us, or show us, who they are. And when they do, we—workers, students, academics, writers, the public—are all accountable to determine if we can live with the current reality or if we must shift the very foundations beneath our museums, so something (or some *things*) wholly new can emerge.

Resistance to an Existential Shift

The International Council of Museums (ICOM) museum definition controversy unfolded in earnest in 2019 and continued as a backdrop to all that has faced the global museum field in the months that followed, coinciding with the COVID-19 pandemic. The struggle of ICOM membership and leadership to come to an agreement about what a museum is and should be is fittingly reflective of the tensions facing the field today. An Inclusive Museum Movement, which we discussed in chapters 1 and 2, continues to grow at the same time as a conservative and wealthy donor class, often linked to corporate interests, maintains influence and power, most notably in the United States's oldest and most resourced museum institutions. In particular, the influence of oil industry–generated wealth in large art museums across the country has continued to attract scrutiny in light of those companies' legacies of community and environmental harms (Yoder, 2019). The conversations that the field has been having over the past several decades, as discussed in chapter 1, have reflected the rise of inclusion discourses and expanded the terrain of possibilities for how we might define museums otherwise. These conversations, and their associated new school of practices and possibilities for museums, gaining in visibility and acceptance for years, may now be on the verge of challenging the nexus of the field's power and identity that has remained resistant to shifting.

In the aspirational openness of the ICOM museum definition put to a vote in Kyoto in 2019, we witness a collective identity claim that emphasizes museums' active role and responsibilities in advancing the ideals of a more inclusive society:

Museums are democratizing, inclusive and polyphonic spaces for critical dialogue about the pasts and the futures. Acknowledging and addressing the conflicts and challenges of the present, they hold artefacts and specimens in trust for society, safeguard diverse memories for future generations and guarantee equal rights and equal access to heritage for all people.

Museums are not for profit. They are participatory and transparent, and work in active partnership with and for diverse communities to collect, preserve, research, interpret, exhibit, and enhance understandings of the world, aiming to contribute to human dignity and social justice, global equality and planetary well-being. (ICOM, 2019)

The pushback and critiques that followed, and their ability to halt the actual adoption of the ICOM museum definition in Kyoto, indicate the power of a contingent that fears the acknowledgment of the already shifting possibilities of what it means to be a museum. The new definition is a departure from dominant paradigms for what is, and should be, at the center of the work that museums do in society. The new definition, should it have been adopted, offered a framework for opening up our understanding of what museums can and should do and suggested all museums demonstrate their relevance in a new way—defined value-first rather than function-first. So far, the events leading up to the introduction of the next ICOM museum definition tell the story of a field constrained yet on the verge of value-centered reimagination.

Care-Centered Critiques

The past couple years have seen a growing field-wide dialogue that draws on the language and the concerns of care ethics. Care ethics is a feminist framework for understanding morality and decision making rooted in relationships and contextual approaches therein. While not new, the sentiment that "museums care more for collections than for people"—including the workers, as well as the communities for which museums hold cultural heritage and material culture in trust—has been a widely expressed conclusion voiced by museum workers at a loss for how else to explain mass layoffs, communication failures, the pushback to labor organizing, and failures to respond to racial injustices in the workplace.

There are many ways in which stories of museum worker experiences and labor organizing struggles were disseminated in 2020 and 2021 and found field-wide audiences. These included:

- staff open letters;
- museum union Instagram and Twitter accounts and websites;
- stories about labor organizing, layoffs, racism, and staff conflicts with leadership reported in *Hyperallergic, The Art Newspaper,* and *ARTnews*; and
- *Change the Museum*—also an Instagram account.

Personal accounts of racism experienced in the workplace have also continued to be highlighted and shared widely, via platforms like Instagram and *Medium* and by art workers, curators, and academics such as La Tanya Autry, Chaédria LaBouvier, Andrea Montiel de Shuman, Dr. Kelli Morgan, and Adrianne Russell. This (nonexhaustive) group of individuals have shared their stories of being failed by their institutions at great risk to themselves. The lengths that cultural workers have gone to relay their stories to the public, and organize for better working conditions and pay through unionizing, illustrates how critical it is that museums strengthen care competencies, care practices, and accountability to care-oriented structures.

In 2020, in the early days of museums responding to the COVID-19 pandemic, Dina Bailey wrote a short article titled "Tomorrow's Normal: The Need for Trauma-Informed Approaches":

> As those in positions of influence make plans for re-opening, and post-opening, I implore everyone to be actively developing trauma-informed approaches—not just considering the physically safest and most expedient way to open sites with the least amount of liability. Trauma-informed approaches will make spaces safer for both staff and visitors by emphasizing the physical, psychological, and emotional safety of everyone. In order to do this, leaders should develop a foundational understanding of what trauma is and how it manifests in individuals and groups. (2020)

Here, Bailey discusses the need for trauma-informed practices precipitated by the COVID-19 pandemic and how existing systemic inequities "leave some groups more vulnerable to trauma . . . and, others more protected from it" (2020). Trauma-informed care now continues to permeate discourse in the arts, heritage, and culture institution landscape. This long overdue turn draws our attention toward the timely care needs we now have in response to a global pandemic, but it also gives us language and a framework to name persisting traumas that the field has left unaddressed for far too long, those connected with systemic oppression perpetuated within, and by, our institutions.

In one targeted action that addressed the widening care gap experienced by laid-off museum workers, Museum Workers Speak (#MWS, also discussed in chapter 1), founded many years prior, launched a mutual aid project to respond to laid-off museum workers in the wake of the pandemic. The scale of need was so great it led #MWS to conclude that "it has become clear to us that when our institutions will not stand in solidarity with us, we must stand in solidarity with one another" (*#MuseumsWorkersSpeak*, 2020). This example demonstrates that, while museum workers have been seeking solidarity in the exchange of their experiences feeling let down by museums at a time of health, social, and economic crisis, there have also been care-centered actions to materially redistribute resources to those who need them most. The need for such care-centered action further supports that a shared clarity about museums is dawning—that museums are wildly inconsistent in their people-oriented care competency. This realization is perhaps best mirrored by our national racial justice reckoning and uprising, which has indicated the scale of ongoing work we have to do cross-institutionally, and as a nation, to reckon with the legacies of oppressive systems like White supremacy. And these are only our most recent indicators of the extent to which the field requires a care-centric values shift. Looking at the care record of museums prior to the past few years further reveals the patterns where the field falls short—the flaws in the design of our current institutional reality.

Museum Legacy Interventions

Running up against departmental and communication silos, gaping wage disparities, gatekeeping, White supremacy, colonialism, and ableism—these were among the ongoing realities for museum workers before the past two years turned lives upside down. Of those many pushing for new ways of working and for the dismantling of broken structures, employment in and under these conditions in museums has required persistence, passion, financial sacrifice, and an unfair share of emotional labor from individuals from historically marginalized groups who are in museum staff and leadership roles. These challenges, as they manifest field-wide and uniquely within each of our respective organizations, demonstrate the gap we have to fill in the field's current understanding, and enacting, of care.

We can learn a lot about the kind(s) of care the museum field has historically prioritized by looking at how curation, and the role of curators, has changed over time. Curators are our museums' most explicitly, eponymously care-oriented role and one that often still holds hierarchical, and symbolic, institutional power. As Aletheia found in her research on the turns from object, to educative, to liberatory-oriented care in museums, "care, as a concept, and curation, as its application in museums, has been constructed through changing museological discourses of how museums should relate to people"

(Wittman, 2017, p. 64). Within the past decade, for instance, we have seen the realm of curatorial practice expand in increasingly community-centered ways and in ways that explicitly engage with social justice. These curatorial practices are still an emerging phenomenon relative to longer-standing ideas of curation and associated practices of care, such as object-oriented care and educative-oriented care that have histories of being tools "used to frame the act of maintaining institutions and their self-interest, consolidating power in dominant cultures and narratives." In the curatorial microcosm of museums, "Room to redefine the practice of curation itself, and invite it to be different based on context and community responsiveness, increasingly directs care and benefits toward people" (2017, p. 64). So at a field-wide level, as well, we must deepen and expand our conceptions of care and dismiss the false binaries of care that hold us back—people care versus collections care and people care versus institutional survival among them.

That museums are overdue to engage with the language and concerns of care ethics head-on is perhaps best illustrated by the fact that there is a growing cohort of museum writers, practitioners, and academics actively developing a discourse of collective, social, and liberatory care paradigms. Dr. Nuala Morse's *The Museum as a Space of Social Care* is a milestone in the scholarship of care ethics and care roles both internal and external to museums and calls for a "care-ful museology" (Morse, 2021). More voices leading the museums and care discourse include La Tanya Autry, Yesumi Umolu, Monica O. Montgomery, Mike Murawski, Museum Workers Speak, and the MASS Action network. And notably, in June 2021, Museums and Race led the "Collective Liberation: Disrupt, Dismantle, Manifest" virtual convening, supported by a newly formed Museum Equity Coalition, members of which include MASS Action, *The Incluseum*, Visitors of Color, The Empathetic Museum, #MWS, Death to Museums, and #museumsarenotneutral. The Museum Equity Coalition itself was a response rooted in a vision of community well-being, collective power, and resource sharing. These individuals, groups, and actions invite us into deeper engagement with care ethics, as they manifest in museums. We might also understand these voices to be forecasting the future (if we want it), part of a relational sea of change—inviting us toward a practice that operates from a place of care-centered values as we detailed in the previous chapter.

We Must Act Before the Cycle of Forgetting Begins Again

As we established in chapter 3, relationships have a special significance in *The Incluseum*'s emergent paradigm for understanding inclusion. Relationships, within this paradigm, are embedded in a web of care-centered values. Relationships are entwined with joint attentiveness to Social Justice, Representation and Access, and Institutional Change. We came to this emergent, relationship-centered paradigm through an analysis of *The Incluseum*'s grassroots digital archive. As an *emergent* paradigm, one might think that all the lessons and insights we have arrived at are radical and new, but "relational practices" are central in teachings that have existed as far back as anyone can remember. Strengthening our field-wide, collective practice of listening to and learning from Indigenous knowledges is key to fostering relational museum practice. As Meredith McCoy, Emma Elliott-Groves, Leilani Sabzalian, and Megan Bang state in their article "Restoring Indigenous Systems of Relationality,"

> Just as Indigenous educational models can serve as a basis for fostering healthier relational practices for all children with each other and the land, so too can Indigenous values serve as a basis for a healthier society. Indigenous knowledge systems and systems of governance are not only relevant to Indigenous peoples, but have relevance and implications for *all* peoples living on Indigenous lands, as well as for the survival of the planet. (2020)

Further, McCoy, Elliott-Groves, Sabzalian, and Bang set forth a vision for our times, responsive to the COVID-19 pandemic and current uprisings against state violence and reliant on our attention to this wisdom: "We imagine a world that fosters stronger human relationships with each other and with the land—the world that we need" (2020). Field-wide there is much to learn from knowledges and frameworks for relationally centered approaches rooted in Indigenous leadership and sovereignty.

While it is clear that museums can react or change under pressure and under public scrutiny, time will tell what is retained from the learning museums are doing now and what lasting transformation has taken place. Many museums made statements that indicated institutional recognition of racism and commitments to address it in the days and weeks after the murder of George Floyd and the start of the racial justice uprising. Far fewer museums have been able to demonstrate they are getting to work putting commitments into practice (MASS Action Accountability Work Group, 2020). Many museums expanded the accessibility of their programming during the COVID-19 pandemic. A recent consultation with D/deaf, disabled, and neurodivergent participants details recommendations about maintaining this momentum in eliminating barriers to engagement, understanding that this progress is fragile and the work far from over (Fox and Sparkes, 2021). At a field-wide scale we need to recognize the threat of forgetting what museums have learned these past two years. New care-centered approaches to inclusion are needed to sustain the momentum of lessons learned and risks taken that have prioritized care for people.

Museums Reimagine Themselves

As detailed in our introduction and chapter 1, *The Incluseum* project has offered a digital platform for community building, amplifying vanguard practices, imagining new ways of being a museum, and chronicling an Inclusive Museum Movement. The emergent paradigm we related in chapter 3 takes as its center the themes of Relationships, Social Justice, Representation and Access, and Institutional Change. The origin of this paradigm, in *The Incluseum*'s digital archive, is an approach to inclusion reflective of grassroots perspectives and practices over a sustained period of time. It is an approach to inclusion that does not presuppose a singular product or solution, but it does insist on openness to transformation.

Museums, as they reacted and responded to a new pandemic reality and shifted content and experience online, showed—if there was any doubt remaining—that they are entirely capable of transformation. *The Incluseum* project, as well, has experienced firsthand that absences of a physical site need not limit your community-building potential. Our time spent weaving webs of content and community online amounted to far more tangible impact—and in-person engagement—than we could have ever predicted. So what is the most integral aspect of being a museum? Is it the building, the physical site, that builds community and sustains it? Our experience with *The Incluseum* tells us that the integral aspects of being a museum need not be so prescribed and static. We believe the most integral traits of museums are embedded in the relational web they weave, the values we stand for, and the power of collaborative inquiry. We believe that is the means by which all museums become *Incluseums*.

A New Paradigm for Inclusion as a Guide on Your Journey

We acknowledge that this work is, and can feel like, a struggle—it can be messy and often places individuals piloting new practices at odds with institutional structures heavily invested in the myth of perfection (Okun, 1999). The tensions of the museum worker experience, rubbing up against a transformation-resistant museum, can feel disheartening, but it does not have to be this way. Grassroots perspectives and ground-up wisdom can be nurtured, and we can build museum cultures that let us all thrive when antiracism is integral to inclusion, as discussed in chapter 2.

Inclusion is a way to clear the overgrowth of oppressive systems, displacing them with systems designed, with care, for all of us.

With support, museum workers that are willing to experiment and take risks in order to enact their own care-centered core values can be an institution's transformation superpower and help museums find their own unique ways forward.

Key Questions

1. Reflect on the strengths and weaknesses of the approach to inclusion that is currently operating at your museum.

   - How would you describe your museum's operating paradigm for inclusion? Is it upholding institutional stasis or helping you transform?
   - What aspects of *The Incluseum*'s paradigm could help mobilize a re-imagining of your museum's future?

2. Assess your museum's past, present, and future relationship accountability.
   - Which of the *Incluseum* paradigm's care-centered values could help ground your assessment of past, present, and future relationships?
   - How could care-centered values illuminate opportunities for relationship repair and healing as we face our museum pasts?

3. Find role models and collaborators.
   - Where are the museums, and other organizations, prioritizing Relationships, Social Justice, Representation and Access, and Institutional Change in your area?
   - How might you connect with these peers as partners in responding to the ongoing, pervasive challenges facing our society and communities?

4. Reconnect to each other in explicitly care-centered ways.
   - How will you emerge as a more care-centered organization from the days of peak pandemic isolation and ongoing pandemic realities?
   - What needs to change about current connecting practices to move toward care-centered connecting?

5. Dismantle systemic inequity.
   - How can Relationships, Social Justice, Representation and Access, and Institutional Change be used to evaluate the fairness of resource distribution that our museums engage in?
   - How can museums respond to embedded inequity by generating new care-centered value-informed structures—from budgets, to policies, to processes?

6. Assess your collections and exhibitions priorities.
   - How might your care for collections evolve when you apply the lens of Relationships, Social Justice, Representation and Access, and Institutional Change?
   - Where is there exhibition alignment with care-centered values, from content to process, and where is there work to do?

7. Open up museum practice to transformation.
   - What care-centered values could you embody to help you weather future storms?
   - How can a focus on Relationships, Social Justice, Representation and Access, and Institutional Change be used to ground a reimagining of your museum?

Bibliography

Autry, La Tanya. "About." *Black Liberation Center*, 2020. https://www.blackliberation center.com/about.

———. "A Black Curator Imagines Otherwise." *Hyperallergic*, April 22, 2021. https://hyperllergic.com/639570/a-black-curator-imagines-otherwise-latanya-autry/.

Bailey, Dina. "Tomorrow's Normal: The Need for Trauma-Informed Approaches." *Informal Learning Review*, Special Issue 2020 #2. https://informallearning.com/storage/issues/ILR-Special-Issue-2020-2.pdf.

Brown, Kate. "What Defines a Museum?" *Artnet*, August 10, 2020. https://news.artnet.com/art-world/icom-museums-definition-resignation-1900194.

Costello, Amy, and Frederica Boswell. "Curator Says It's Time to Tackle the Art World's Racist Culture." *Nonprofit Quarterly*, March 11, 2021. https://nonprofitquarterly.org/curator-says-its-time-to-tackle-the-art-worlds-racist-culture/.

Durón, Maximiliano, and Alex Greenberger. "In Open Letters, Art Workers Demand that Institutions Do More to Fight Racism." *ARTnews*, June 19, 2020. https://www.artnews.com/art-news/news/art-workers-systemic-racism-open-letters-1202691764/.

Fox, Esther, and Jane Sparkes. "Curating for Change: Disabled People Leading in Museums." 2021. http://www.accentuateuk.org/?location_id=5034.

Holmes, Helen. "The Guggenheim's First Black Curator Is Denouncing the Museum's Treatment of Her." *Observer*, 2020. https://observer.com/2020/06/guggenheim-museum-chaedria-labouvier/.

"ICOM Announces the Alternative Museum Definition That Will Be Put to a Vote." ICOM. 2019. https://icom.museum/en/news/icom-announces-the-alternative-museum-definition-that-will-be-subject-to-a-vote/.

Kendall Adams, Geraldine. "Ideological Rift Persists as ICOM Restarts Museum Definition Consultation." Museum Association, March 2, 2021. https://www.museumsassociation.org/museums-journal/news/2021/03/ideological-rift-persists-as-icom-restarts-museum-definition-consultation/.

MASS Action Accountability Work Group. "From Solidarity to Transformative Action and Accountability." 2020. https://www.museumaction.org/massaction-blog/2020/8/31/from-statements-of-solidarity-to-transformative-action-amp-accountability.

McCoy, Meredith, Emma Elliott-Groves, Leilani Sabzalian, and Megan Bang. "Restoring Indigenous Systems of Relationality." Center for Humans and Nature, October 7, 2020. https://www.humansandnature.org/restoring-indigenous-systems-of-relationality.

Montiel de Shuman, Andrea. "No Longer in Extremis." *Medium*, June 15, 2020. https://medium.com/@andreamontiel23/no-longer-in-extremis-9aa1c5996f35.

Morse, Nuala. *The Museum as a Space of Social Care*. New York: Routledge, 2021.

Murawski, Mike. *Museums as Agents of Change*. Lanham, MD: Rowman & Littlefield, 2021.

"Museum Workers Speak Website Statement." 2020. https://sites.google.com/view/museumworkersspeak/.

Okun, Tema. "White Supremacy Culture." 1999. https://www.dismantlingracism.org/uploads/4/3/5/7/43579015/okun_-_white_sup_culture.pdf.

Umolu, Yesumi. "On the Limits of Care and Knowledge: 15 Points Museums Must Understand to Dismantle Structural Injustice." *Artnet*, June 25, 2020. https://news.artnet.com/opinion/limits-of-care-and-knowledge-yesomi-umolu-op-ed-1889739.

Wittman, Aletheia. "Expanding Care: Curation in the Age of Engagement." *FWD:Museums*, no. 2 (2017): 64–75.

Yoder, Kate. "The Art of Oil." *Grist*, December 18, 2019. https://grist.org/climate/can-art-museums-survive-without-oil-money/.

5

Future Visioning

IN APRIL 2020, Arundhati Roy's thought-provoking piece "The Pandemic Is a Portal," a response to the impact of COVID-19 in India, went viral for this assertion:

> Historically, pandemics have forced humans to break with the past and imagine their world anew. This one is no different. It is a portal, a gateway between one world and the next. We can choose to walk through it, dragging the carcasses of our prejudice and hatred, our avarice, our data banks and dead ideas, our dead rivers and smoky skies behind us. Or we can walk through lightly, with little luggage, ready to imagine another world. And ready to fight for it.

Stepping through a portal necessarily changes how we perceive reality. For example, things that might have been obfuscated are now crystal clear. Going through this "pandemic as portal," we see even more clearly that systems are in need of overhaul. This is the case for our museums, especially when considering the value of inclusion. But, as Roy writes, we can imagine another world, and this is what the analysis of our decade-long process of collaborative inquiry, about what inclusion is and can be, proposes—imagining other worlds. In this journey of imagining otherwise, we have the opportunity to expand, and possibly upend in surprising ways, our understandings of museums, inclusion, and ourselves.

In an interview for The Man Enough Podcast, gender-nonconforming author, performer, speaker, fashionista, and activist Alok Vaid-Menon implores us to reframe our binary thinking and go deeper. Rather than think in binaries of "us and them," which are deeply othering, they ask us to interrogate the ways we frame issues in terms of how we can help "the other." Their argument is that all oppression is connected and that when we think in dichotomies—as if the oppression is outside of ourselves—we hinder our very own growth and learning. Alok's work teaches us that when we listen to and promote the research, contributions, and activism of the people of the global majority who work in and lead our field, we allow for the honesty of those who experience the "brunt of the collected fantasies that are created" to be heard. When we fight for equity, access, and justice for one, we fight for these things for ourselves. Alok asks us to consider mightily, "Are you ready to heal?"

This work—the work of inclusion and all that it entails—is everyone's responsibility, not just that of the director of inclusion, the inclusion catalyst, the director of equity and inclusion, BIPOC staff, or the CEO of belonging and engagement. Understanding and enacting inclusion is an ongoing endeavor that helps all of us challenge our current realities to forge new futures. Indeed, inclusion opens us up to the emergent and pluralistic possibilities of transformation so we can exude completely new, always evolving, and unique ways of being a museum.

We honor the work of all those who have worked hard on behalf of transformative inclusion over the past decade (and beyond). We know that we will continue to need new and evolving approaches to inclusion on the journey ahead. The insights we have compiled and shared in this book highlight how inclusion itself continues to transform in light of the growth made possible through collaborative inquiry and collective wisdom. The museum field's early use of the term "inclusion" opened the door for ongoing inquiry about the limits and possibilities of this concept and associated practices. As we have demonstrated in this book, the meanings inclusion holds today encompass a continuously unfolding terrain that recognizes racial justice and care-centered values as central tenets. Additionally, as we discussed in chapter 4, the realities of the COVID-19 global pandemic are now prompting further inquiry and revaluation of our approaches to inclusion.

Taking the time for the excavation of inclusion expanded, and continues to expand, our imaginations and the horizons beyond where any of us might have dreamed the field would be. In doing so, we have collectively gone where Stephen Weil (1999) directed us to and yet still have much farther to travel. The past ten years of working with *The Incluseum* project has shown us the power of collaborative inquiry as a means of leading us forward, in pursuit of collective wisdom, in this next phase of museum transformation. This process of inquiring collaboratively was of utmost importance to us, for as social justice facilitator adrienne maree brown states,

In order to create a world that works for more people, for more life, we have to collaborate on the process of dreaming and visioning and implementing that world. We have to recognize that a multitude of realities have, do, and will exist. (2017, p. 158)

In this book we have set out to show what we have learned about inclusion from *The Incluseum* project:

- Inclusion is a collaborative, multimodal, expansive, and inquisitive process (introduction).
- Inclusion is a developing discourse, descended from, and related to, many connected efforts over time (chapter 1).
- Inclusion can't exist without antiracism (chapter 2).
- Inclusion is about care-centered relationships that center social justice to increase representation and access to museum resources and hinges on institutional change (chapter 3).
- Inclusion is a way to clear the overgrowth of oppressive systems, displacing them with systems designed, with care, for all of us (chapter 4).

Accordingly, the ways we work to *be inclusive* require a paradigm shift moving forward. Imagine the future state you are trying to embody. What does it sound like? What does it feel like? What does it taste like? What would the museum field, our cities and towns, look like if filled with *Incluseums*? **What kind of Incluseum will you be?** We all have a role in forecasting this reality. Consider the world-building potential of:

- values-led practice;
- practice and process over product;
- inquiry over answers, especially prescriptive ones;
- care, imagination, and experimentation-informed metrics; and
- building community hand in hand with a building in the community.

We recognize these insights are not definitive. We have focused primarily on the US landscape because of the context of our work and organizing, however this is a global conversation in need of more global perspectives and web weaving. *The Incluseum* project has also by no means exhaustively engaged with all the rich and urgent discourses in the field today. The beauty of collaborative inquiry is that there will *always* be new ideas and practices by which to complicate, nuance, enrich, and further our understanding of inclusion. The beauty of a new and emergent paradigm for understanding inclusion is that we do not need to have all the answers but instead must be open to critical questions and ultimately to *the assurance* of transformation. Inclusion is a beginning instead of an end.

The Incluseum

Key Questions

1. Dream your *Incluseum*. Draw it. Sketch it. Record a short video or audio clip. What are the best parts about your *Incluseum* that you can share? Tag us on any social media platform you are on.
2. Where are museums headed next? What's your role in this work?
3. What can you do now to support dynamic individuals, organizations, institutions, etc. that are doing the work well?
4. How can you harness the powers of digital connectivity and collaborative inquiry to advance transformation and change?

Bibliography

brown, adrienne maree. *Emergent Strategy: Shaping Change, Changing Worlds.* Chico, CA: AK Press, 2017.

Roy, Arundhati. "The Pandemic Is a Portal." *Financial Times*, April 3, 2020. https://www.ft.com/content/10d8f5e8-74eb-11ea-95fe-fcd274e920ca.

Vaid-Menon, Alok. "The Urgent Need for Compassion." The Man Enough Podcast, July 16, 2021. https://www.youtube.com/watch?v=Tq3C9R8HNUQ.

Weil, Stephen. "From Being about Something to Being for Somebody: The Ongoing Transformation of the American Museum." *Daedalus* 128, no. 3 (1999): 229–58.

Appendix

TABLE 6.1 INCLUDES all the blogposts that were included in the analysis presented in chapter 3. Because Rose's research took place in the spring of 2020, she considered all blogposts published up to that time. *The Incluseum* has continued to publish content since the spring of 2020; as such, this table is not exhaustive. We honor and are grateful to all authors who have collaborated with *The Incluseum* since 2012. The breadth and depth of their collective work is rich and truly inspirational.

Table 6.1

Blogpost Title	Author(s)	Year
Setting the Stage Part 1: About This Blog and Defining "Social Inclusion"	Rose Paquet and Aletheia Wittman	2012
Setting the Stage Part 2: About This Blog and Defining "Social Inclusion"	Rose Paquet and Aletheia Wittman	2012
The Whatcom Museum Serves Homeless Adults and Families	Mary-Jo Maute; Rose Paquet (interviewer)	2012
Facing Homelessness: Skid Road at [Storefront], Olson Kundig Architects	Aletheia Wittman	2012
Comfort and Connectivity: The Museum as Healer	Anne Melton	2012
Creating a Community-Based Music Exhibition	Leen Rhee	2012
Queer Is Here and in Our Museums!	Erin Bailey	2012
The Pop-Up Museum as a Social Inclusion Strategy	Michelle Delcarlo	2012
Creating Museum Programs with Adults Experiencing Poverty	Emily Leighton	2012
Seattle's First Arts and Social Change Symposium	Rose Paquet and Aletheia Wittman	2012
Pullman Porter Blues: Voices Amplified	Brian Carter; Aletheia Wittman (interviewer)	2012
Multimodal Approaches to Learning Conferences: Reflections	Jamie Walsh	2012
Can Exhibit Be Allies? Part 1	Diana Falchuk	2012
Can Exhibit Be Allies? Part 2	Diana Falchuk	2012
Youth and Community Outreach at the Seattle's EMP Museum	Jonathan Cunningham; Rose Paquet and Aletheia Wittman (interviewers)	2012
Including Museums in Critical Mixed-Race Studies	Chieko Phillips	2012
Allyship and the Race Exhibit: Reflections Part I	Robert Garfinkle	2012
Museums and Children with Autism Spectrum Disorders	Rose Paquet and Aletheia Wittman	2012
Promoting Artists of All Abilities: The Quickest Flip Project	Jamie Walsh	2012
Allyship and the Race Exhibit: Reflections Part 2	Robert Garfinkle	2012
Reflections on Our "Race in the Museum" Mixer	Rose Paquet and Aletheia Wittman	2012
A Museum as a Stage for Dialogue: Expanding Museum Communities with Programming for International Refugees	Tara Lyons	2013
Announcing www.autisminthemuseum.org: A Growing Online Clearinghouse of Ideas, Resources, Models, and Information for Inclusion and Access	Lisa Jo Rudy	2013
"What's It Like [. . .] in Morrison County?": Toward a More Inclusive Representation of History	Mary Warner	2013

(continued)

Table 6.1. *(continued)*

Blogpost Title	Author(s)	Year
The Danger of the "D" Word: Museums and Diversity	Porchia Moore	2014
A Family's First Ticket to a Lifetime of Learning	Candice Anderson	2014
Shifting Paradigms: The Case for Co-Creation and New Discourses of Participation	Porchia Moore	2014
The Road to Revealing Queer: An Interview with Curator Erin Bailey, Part 1	Erin Bailey; Jana Greenslit (interviewer)	2014
The Road to Revealing Queer: An Interview with Curator Erin Bailey, Part 2	Erin Bailey; Jana Greenslit (interviewer)	2014
Re-Thinking Narrative Productions in Museums through Digital Storytelling Workshops	Nicole Robert	2014
The Museum as Kaleidoscope	Porchia Moore	2014
(Re)Connection in Collaboration: Zuni Collections Reviews at the Indian Arts Research Center	Patricia Baudino	2014
Radical Trust	Porchia Moore	2014
Rethinking Museum Jobs at the Museum of Art and History in Santa Cruz, CA	Rose Paquet	2014
Seven Ways to Make the Museum System a Better Place for People of Color	Hannah Hong	2014
Exhibit Opening: An Introduction to the Power of Labeling	Rose Paquet and Aletheia Wittman	2014
Including the 21st Century Family	Margaret Middleton	2014
Cross-Institutional Partnerships: Opportunities for Inclusion	Porchia Moore	2014
Repatriating Knowledge: Connecting Museums and Communities Part 1	Sven Haakanson Jr.; Rose Paquet (interviewer)	2014
Repatriating Knowledge: Connecting Museums and Communities Part 2	Sven Haakanson Jr.	2014
Pop-Up Museums in Santa Cruz	Nora Grant	2014
AAM's Diversity and Inclusion Policy Statement Part 1	Auntaneshia Staveloz; William Harris; Rose Paquet (interviewer)	2014
AAM's Diversity and Inclusion Policy Statement Part 2	Auntaneshia Staveloz; William Harris; Rose Paquet (interviewer)	2014
We Can't Outsources Empathy Part 1: Thoughts on AAM's Diversity and Inclusion Policy	Gretchen Jennings	2014
We Can't Outsources Empathy Part 2: Thoughts on AAM's Diversity and Inclusion Policy	Gretchen Jennings	2014

Title	Author(s)	Year
4 Steps for Successful Museum Social Work	Zachary Stocks	2014
Museumopplis: Teens Research and Prototype Museums of the Future	Aletheia Wittman	2014
Social Justice Alliance of Museums (SJAM)	David Fleming	2014
Incluseum Design Session with Museum of Northwest Art	Aletheia Wittman	2014
Responding to the Events in Ferguson and Beyond: The Northwest African American Museum's Example	Chieko Phillips and Leilani Lewis	2014
Joint Statement from Museum Bloggers and Colleagues on Ferguson and Related Events	Aleia Brown, Elisa Granata, Gretchen Jennings, Steven Lubar, Maragret Middleton, Porchia Moore, Mike Murawski, Linda Norris, Paul Orselli, Rose Paquet, Ed Rodley, Adrianne Russell, Nina Simon, nikhil trivedi, Rainey Tisdale, Jeanne Vergeront, and Aletheia Wittman	2014
"Radio Magica Libera Tutti!": An Innovative and Inclusive Project to Guarantee Children Playful Digital Accessibility to the Artistic Heritage of the Veneto Region	Elena Rocco	2014
Racial Equity Resources	Rose Paquet	2014
Twitter Chat: #museumsrespondtoferguson	Aleia Brown and Andrianne Russell	2015
Oprresion: A Museum Primer	nikhil trivedi	2015
Introducing Museum of Impact	Monica Montgomery	2015
Discovering Our Inclusion Model: The National Public Housing Museum	Daniel Ronan	2015
Museums and the Reproduction of Disadvantage	Emily Dawson	2015
Why Think About Equity and Museums?	Emily Dawson	2015
Challenging Oppression in Museums	Emily Dawson	2015
Incluseum Tour Notes on the Indigenous Beauty Exhibit	Aletheia Wittman	2015
High Art Connect: Blogging for Social Engagement at the High Museum of Art	Nina Pelaez	2015
Pre-Conference Dialogue on the AAM Diversity and Inclusion Policy Statement	Timothy Hecox, Rose Paquet, Cecile Shellman, Virgil Talaid, and Aletheia Wittman	2015
Announcing the Department of Inclusion and Community Engagement at the Minnesota Historical Society Part 1	Chris Taylor	2015

(continued)

Table 6.1. *(continued)*

Blogpost Title	Author(s)	Year
Announcing the Department of Inclusion and Community Engagement at the Minnesota Historical Society Part 2	Chris Taylor	2015
For the Love of Al Green: Revisiting Bunch's "Flies in the Buttermilk" 15 Years Later	Porchia Moore	2015
How Do We Turn the Social Justice Lens Inward? A Conversation about Internal Museum Labor Practices	Alyssa Greenberg	2015
Reflecting on AAM	Margaret Middleton, Porchia Moore, and Rose Paquet	2015
Michelle Obama, "Activism," and Museum Employment: Part 1	Porchia Moore, Rose Paquet, and Aletheia Wittman	2015
The Power of Place: A Collaboration with All Rise	Rose Paquet and Aletheia Wittman	2015
Trans Family Photo Gallery Project	Margaret Middleton and Matt Clowney	2015
Michelle Obama, "Activism," and Museum Employment: Part 2	Porchia Moore, Rose Paquet, and Aletheia Wittman	2015
Activist? Activism? Museum?	Porchia Moore and Rose Paquet	2015
An Intercultural Tool for Museums	Hannelore Franck, Yasmine Heynderickx, Anais Masure, and Pierre Tanguay	2015
Incluseum Letter to the Editor in Museum Magazine	Rose Paquet and Aletheia Wittman	2015
Building Community for Lasting Change	Rose Paquet, nikhil trivedi; and Aletheia Wittman	2015
Necessary Force: Art in the Police State at the University of New Mexico Museum of Art	Traci Quinn; Rose Paquet (interviewer)	2015
Queering the Museum Piece in "Storytelling the Experiences of Gender and Sexuality in Museums"	Sarah Olivo	2015
Two Takeaways from Museumnext 2015	Alyssa Greenberg	2015
Diversity and Inclusion in the 21st Century Workshop Reflection	Aletheia Wittman	2015
R-e-s-p-e-c-t! Church Ladies, Magical Negroes, and Model Minorities: Understanding Inclusion from Community to Communities	Porchia Moore	2015
Taboo: Incluseum Edition	Porchia Moore and Rose Paquet	2015

Table 6.1. *(continued)*

Blogpost Title	Author(s)	Year
LACMA Intern Thoughts: Casta Paintings and Some Race Potions	Angela E. Medrano	2017
Sites of Conscience: Truth, Reconciliation, Resistance	Aletheia Wittman	2017
On Creating the Museum of Minneapolis	Jaden Hansen	2017
Letter to Young Museum Professionals of Color or What Transpires on a Long-Haul Career When Confronted with Racism in Museums	Radiah Harper	2017
Whiteness and Museum Education	Hannah Heller	2017
MASS Action 2017 Convening	Aletheia Wittman	2017
I Read to Survive	andrea laroc	2017
Reading for What Is and What Might Be	Therese Quinn	2017
Reading in Troubled Times	Karen Carter	2017
The Dreamspace Project: A Critical Workbook and Toolkit for Critical Praxis in the American Art Museum Part 3	Alyssa Machida	2018
Think/Feel: Towards More Meaningful Encounters with Identity-Based Art	Ariana Lee	2018
Anti-Prison Organizing and Museums: The Politics of Remembering and Forgetting	Therese Quinn, Matthew Yasuoka, Jose Luis Benavides, and Other Members of the Illinois Deaths in Custody Project	2018
Interpreting Slavery in Historic Cities	Rose Paquet	2018
I Am the Person Sitting Next to You	Anonymous	2018
Museopunks Action Recap	nikhil trivedi	2018
The Smithsonian Asian Pacific Center's Cultural Lab Manifesto Playbook	Andrea Kim Neighbors	2018
An Introduction to MASS Action Toolkit from the Co-Founder	Elisabeth Callihan	2018
Expanding Care: Curation in the Age of Engagement	Aletheia Wittman	2019
Factories of Stories	Simona Bodo	2019
Exhibitions for Social Justice	Elena Gonzales	2019
Uncovering White Supremacy Culture in Museum Work	Hannah Heller, nikhil trivedi, and Joanne Jones-Rizzi	2020
Feeling Van Gogh—Making Vincent Van Gogh's Art More Accessible	Harma van Uffelen	2020

Index

Page references for figures are italicized.

About the Authors

Porchia Moore is an innovative thought leader, cultural heritage scholar, outdoor enthusiast, writer, artist, curator, and museum consultant specializing in racial equity. She is program head of museum studies at the University of Florida. Porchia has traveled the world visiting and learning from museums and centers the practice teaching to transgress as outlined by Black feminist scholar bell hooks for liberatory education. She cofounded the *Visitors of Color* project with nikhil trivedi and partners with museums across the nation to increase racial literacy, cultural competence, and engaged and empathic praxis. She is codirector of *The Incluseum*. Porchia is committed to creating a world that is verdant, free of anti-Blackness, joy filled, and uplifts the material culture and world heritage of all peoples.

Rose Paquet is a public scholar, artist, coach, and facilitator. She works with people to use the power of the imagination to dream and enact future possibilities that center community care in its widest understanding—care for the body and soul, care for both human and nonhuman kin, care for the soil beneath our feet, the air we breathe, and the water we drink. Rose cofounded *The Incluseum* in 2012 and currently acts as codirector. She completed her PhD in information science from the University of Washington in 2021. Rose has been working with museums for the past eighteen years and has been particularly shaped by her experiences at the Alutiiq Museum and Archaeological Repository in Kodiak, Alaska, where she supported projects of cultural repatriation.

Aletheia Wittman is a facilitator, consultant, coach, and writer. She works with individuals and groups as a partner in the processes of inclusive transformation and institutional genealogy. Aletheia's practice is grounded in values of creativity, curiosity, and collective care. Her research and writing focus on museum legacies, enacting care in museums, as well as power dynamics in contemporary museum culture. In addition to consulting projects with cultural organizations across the United States, she continues to work in and with cultural organizations in the Pacific Northwest, where she has lived for over a decade. Aletheia cofounded *The Incluseum* in 2012 and currently acts as codirector. She holds a graduate degree in museology from the University of Washington (2012), where she researched emerging curatorial practice in art museums and how those practices engage with social justice issues.